Geraldene Holt's

COUNTRY HOUSE
COOKING

Geraldene Holt's

COUNTRY HOUSE
COOKING

RECIPES FOR BOTH STOVES AND
TRADITIONAL RANGES

B⊞XTREE

For my mother and my daughter,

with love

ACKNOWLEDGEMENTS

I thank Michael Alcock for inviting me to write this book and my editor, Vicky Monk, who has been conscientious and considerate in keeping me to the schedule. At Spillers of Chard, Christine and Andrew Durie, and Jacqueline Bond have been keen on this book from the outset and I am grateful for their support and for their cheerful Aga maintenance team. Thanks, too to Kit Johnson for the sympathetic design of the book and to James Murphy for the superb way he always photographs my food. I am grateful to Amanda Evans, formerly editor of *Homes & Gardens* magazine, for encouraging me to write about my cooking in Devon. My good friend and neighbour Gwen Tidball, who grew up cooking over an open fire and on a range has given me years of valuable advice and many memories of country life. Lastly, I thank my mother for her love of cooking and for the good food she has always provided.

First published in Great Britain in 1996
by Boxtree Limited, Broadwall House, 21 Broadwall, London SE1 9PL

Copyright © Geraldene Holt 1996

The right of Geraldene Holt to be identified as Author
of this work has been asserted by her in accordance with the Copyright,
Designs and Patents Act 1988

ISBN 0 7522 0506 4

Designed by Kit Johnson
Photographs by James Murphy

Typeset by Dorchester Typesetting
Printed and bound by Butler & Tanner Ltd, Frome and London

A CIP catalogue entry for this book is available from the British Library

Contents

~

INTRODUCTION

It's intriguing why many of us find the
deep, concentrated flavours that
food develops in oven cooking are so
pleasurable and satisfying – it's
as if hidden in our genes are encoded
memories of how food used to
taste. No other style of cooking
captivates the palate in quite the
same way bringing that sense of total
contentment that only good food
can instil.

Left
SAFFRON ORZO *page 56*

As I THREW another log on the fire just now, it occurred to me that the wood fire in this house has burned – more or less constantly – for centuries. Upstairs, you can still see its ancient soot on the medieval beams, and the layer of hard, gleaming tar in the chimney is inches thick.

For most of its history the cooking here has been done over this same hearth fire in the wide inglenook. Huge joints of meat were roasted on a revolving spit close to the flames, and heavy black cauldrons of soup and stew were suspended over the fire from the iron rod fixed across the throat of the chimney. Bread was baked on a bake stone in the hearth until the seventeenth century when the brick-lined beehive bread oven was constructed to one side of the fireplace.

Early in the nineteenth century, a revolutionary new cast-iron range was installed in the flagstoned kitchen. All over Britain, at that time, cast-iron ranges were fitted into the big old fireplaces. Their style varied with the region; in Devon and Cornwall, the open fire, contained by bars at the front, heated a side oven with its upper surface forming a hot plate or hob. A later refinement was a range with a small water boiler, set either close to the oven or on the other side of the firebasket. The introduction of the cast-iron range opened up far wider possibilities for the cook; and so the style of elegant English cooking, described in 1845 by Eliza Acton in *Modern Cookery for Private Families*, with its repertoire of subtly-flavoured dishes and carefully cooked sauces, became feasible in many country houses.

In time, though, the limitations of the old iron range became all too apparent: its heat was still largely subject to the wayward draught in the chimney and the stove's maintenance was arduous and time-consuming with its regular application of black-leading, necessary to prevent corrosion.

And so, about fifty years ago, the much-improved descendant of the Victorian range was installed in our kitchen. By now, the stove's cast-iron case was coated with easy-to-clean vitreous enamel, the source of heat was totally enclosed, and the superior insulation retained the heat, making it far more efficient. My present version runs on electricity with a clever box of electronics that makes the stove highly responsive, it provides continuous heat for my cooking and for the comfort of the whole house.

When I think of the food that has been prepared, cooked, and eaten in this house over hundreds of years, I am aware that I am part of that country tradition. I count myself blessed that I've lived most of my life in the country, growing much of my own food, and cooking in traditional style on an Aga cooker. I was brought up to cook this way – on what Elizabeth David called 'a proper stove' – following the pattern set by my mother, my grandmother, and even my great-grandmother, all of whom took a pride in cooking well and serving fine English food.

This ribbon of continuity threads its way through the kind of food I cook. Some of my recipes have been handed down from my family – annotated as 'very good' in old cookery books, or carefully described in yellowing, kitchen-stained notepads, or just scribbled on scraps of paper. A century or so ago, this book itself would have been a manuscript – penned in copperplate – to be handed on to my daughter. But most of the recipes here are ones that I devise as I cook, they are part of the record I keep of dishes that, to me, have value beyond the meal ahead and are worthy of being cooked again and again. Though often informed by the past, my cooking is primarily inspired by the ingredients themselves: fresh, peerless produce from our garden and orchard, from local farms and hillsides, nearby rivers and the sea. For genuine country house cooking with its beautiful, unpretentious style derives from its locality.

Of course, I am privileged to be able to cook this way – the way everyone once did – rather than having to depend upon the city supermarket's exotica and weekly price reductions. I'm able to do this because, twenty years ago, my husband and I decided to move with our children, into this old farmhouse in the heart of the Devon countryside, to live as self-sufficiently as possible. And though at times life has been quite hard, it has also brought us fulfilment, good health and happiness.

We moved here for a rural life in a kind climate. Yet, in spite of the historic blizzards, droughts and storms that have at times assailed us, we could not have chosen a more favoured land. For during the last decade or so, Devon has seen a small army of growers, farmers, millers and cheese-makers arrive to practise sustainable agriculture, and point the way forward for decent, home-grown British food that we can trust.

Before I began to write about food I was a potter, and when I fired my kilns I needed to know what temperatures they reached. To do this, I used a thermocouple and also ceramic cones which bend over when they reach a certain temperature. A kiln is, at its simplest, an oven for pots, which may be why I always cook with thermometers to hand. In the following recipes, which are specially suited to oven cooking, I give the desired cooking temperatures for whatever system you use – a traditional multi-fuel range or a conventional gas or electric cooker.

But so that you can cook from this book with confidence, I would advise you to acquire a small inexpensive oven thermometer to determine what temperature your oven(s) reaches and how it may vary – from top to bottom or front to back. For – just like people – cooking stoves can be highly individual, so a kitchen notebook for jotting down your observations of cooking temperatures and times helps to ensure that dishes turn out as intended.

The gloriously rich flavours of roasting and baking characteristic of traditional country cooking are simple to achieve, and yet delight and satisfy. Few would deny the appeal of such good things as freshly-baked soda bread, cocotte eggs gently set in the oven with thick cream and fresh herbs, onions slowly braised in wine, a perfectly simple roast chicken, and a golden marmalade pudding glistening with its own zesty sauce. This is my kind of country cooking.

CLYST WILLIAM BARTON, DEVON.

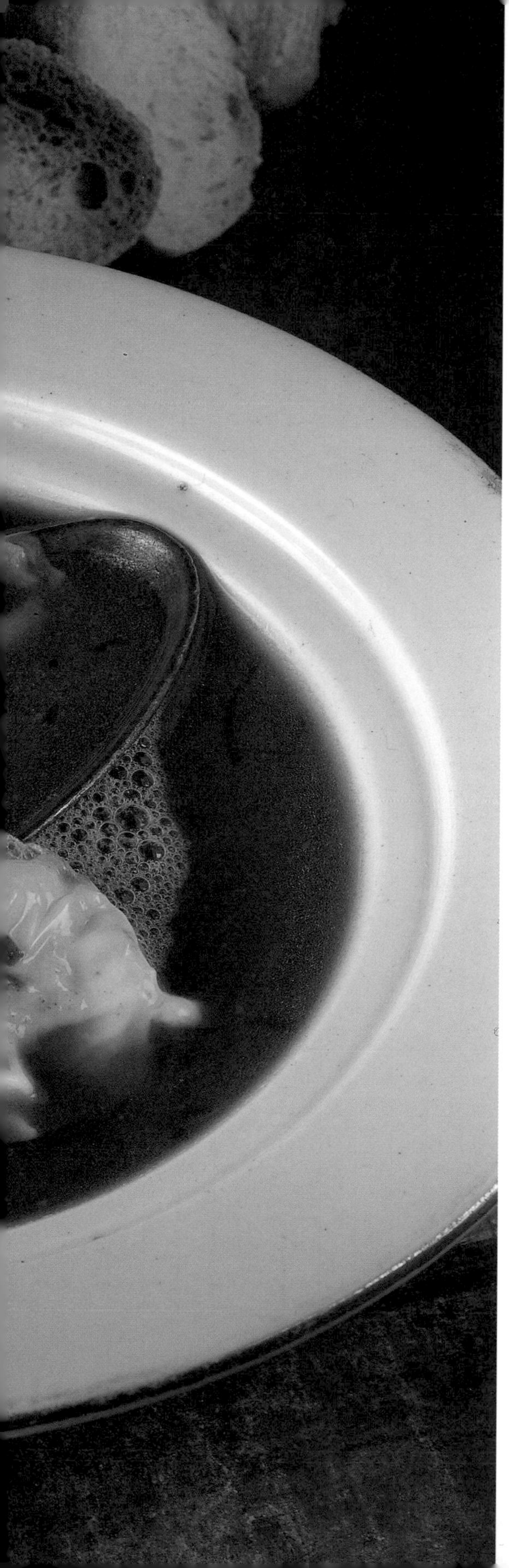

CHAPTER 1

SOUPS AND FIRST COURSES

Just as in music, an overture to a meal should be a well-judged part of the whole composition: the first course should be an appetizing foretaste or a pleasing counterpoint to the food to follow.

Left
PROVENÇAL FISH SOUP WITH *ROUILLE* *page 13*

PRECIOUS spears of April asparagus or the earliest picking of tender spring vegetables – just enough for modest servings – are best served in pride of place, at the start. And because a first course is served in small portions it should be utterly distinctive in taste and appearance, an irresistible invitation to commence the meal.

In the country, a bowl of soup is still the most traditional way to start an evening meal – indeed, supper itself takes its name from the dish. This age-old custom of appeasing our hunger with a richly-flavoured hot liquid has great merit: for a nourishing soup, sipped slowly to appreciate its flavour, both pleases the palate and allows the digestion proper time to adjust to eating. A simple aromatic broth is more comforting and soothing than almost any other dish in the English kitchen. And when – particularly in cold weather – it is crammed with goodness in the form of chopped vegetables, slivers of chicken, game or ham, and a handful of pearl barley or rice, then a generous serving of soup provides a light meal in itself.

Unless you run a large household – or are supremely well-organized – gone are the days when a stockpot was a constant burbling companion in every kitchen. However, when time allows and especially if you cook on a range, it makes good sense to utilize any meat bones, or a poultry carcase, or just the peelings and trimmings from fresh vegetables, to make a foundation for soups. Simply pile the ingredients into a casserole, add a bouquet of garden herbs, an onion, a stick of celery, and a dried mushroom or two. Cover with cold water and slowly bring to the boil. Place on a tight-fitting lid and simmer in the oven for 1 hour. Strain the stock and taste, and if too watery, concentrate its flavour by boiling fast over high heat until reduced in volume. Use freshly-made stock straight away for making soup, or chill and freeze until needed. Of course, many excellent soups do not require stock, they are simply based on a well-flavoured purée of vegetables or fish, thinned to a pouring consistency with cream, milk, yoghurt or wine.

A good soup has a definite identity, with a flavour and texture that is immediately appealing. Yet even a worthy but dull soup can often be improved in a matter of moments: a few leaves of chopped tarragon or chives stirred into the simmering brew, or a judicious splash of sherry or Madeira – even sloe gin or whisky – can supply the necessary extra depth of flavour. Or just taking the trouble to sieve a puréed soup until velvety-smooth, or adding a crust of crisp pastry to a tureen of soup, can produce a memorably delicious dish to open the meal.

PROVENÇAL FISH SOUP WITH *ROUILLE*

A fine Provençal soup that dispels the gloom of a winter's day.

SERVES 4

2-3 tablespoons olive oil

1 onion, chopped

1-2 cloves of garlic, peeled and chopped

680 g / 1½ lb mixed bony fish pieces, preferably flat white fish

225 g / 8 oz tomatoes, peeled and chopped

bouquet garni of fresh parsley, thyme, piece of celery and a bay leaf

1 litre / 1¾ pints water

150 ml / 5 fl oz good red wine from Provence

salt, few black peppercorns

½ teaspoon strands of saffron

Pernod to taste

ROUILLE

1 small fresh, or ½ a dried, hot red chilli, deseeded

1-2 cloves garlic, peeled

¼ teaspoon sea salt

2-3 rounded tablespoons mayonnaise

¼ teaspoon tomato purée (optional)

slices of French baguette, toasted to make *croûtes*

85 g / 3 oz Gruyère cheese, finely grated

OVEN

180°C 350°F Gas Mark 4 Simmering Oven

Heat the oil in a large casserole, stir in the onion and garlic and cook until softened. Add the fish and quickly turn it over in the oil. Add the tomatoes, bouquet garni, water, wine, salt and peppercorns, and bring to the boil. Cover and cook in the preheated oven for 30 minutes.

Strain the soup through a sieve, pressing the fish gently to extract the full flavour. Return the liquid to the pan, add the saffron and simmer for 20 minutes until the flavour and colour has been extracted from the spice. Taste and adjust the seasoning of the soup. A drop or two of Pernod usually enhances the flavour.

While the soup cooks, prepare the *rouille*: chop the fresh chilli – if using a dried chilli, soften it in a little warm water first – and pound to a purée with the garlic and salt with a pestle and mortar, or in a small blender. Mix in the mayonnaise and, if desired, add the tomato purée to give a good rust-red colour. Spoon the *rouille* into a small dish. Serve the freshly-toasted *croûtes* in a cloth-lined basket, and the grated Gruyère cheese in a small wooden or pottery bowl.

Serve the soup in hot bowls and hand the *rouille*, the *croûtes*, and the cheese round separately. Each person should float a *croûte* or two – covered with *rouille* or cheese or both – on top of the soup, stirring to incorporate the flavours.

Parten Bree or Scottish Crab Broth

*This is a good, simple soup with rich flavour
and smooth, creamy consistency.
When the weather is bitterly cold, a dash of
Scotch whisky added to the soup with the
cream does no harm.*

S E R V E S 4 - 6

55 g / 2 oz pudding rice

600 ml / 1 pint full-cream milk

1 bay leaf

slice of onion

short piece of celery

short piece of cinnamon stick

300 g / 10 oz fresh crab meat

450 ml / 15 fl oz well-flavoured fish or
chicken stock

1 anchovy fillet, pounded to a paste

salt and freshly milled black pepper

150 ml / 5 fl oz double cream

small knob of butter

G A R N I S H

flat-leaf parsley, chopped

O V E N

160°C 325°F Gas Mark 3 Simmering Oven

Measure the rice and milk into a pan, bring
almost to the boil with the bay leaf, onion,
celery and cinnamon. Cover with a lid and
cook in the preheated oven for 20 minutes or
until soft. Remove the bay leaf, onion, celery
and cinnamon and pour the rice and milk
into a processor. Reserve some of the white
crab meat from the claws, add the remaining
crab meat to the processor and blend until
· you have a smooth paste.

Return the puréed mixture to the pan with
the fish stock, add the pounded anchovy and
season to taste with salt and pepper. Stir in
the cream and reserved crab meat, then bring
the soup almost to the boil. Remove from the
heat, add the butter and ladle into hot soup
bowls. Garnish with chopped parsley and
serve immediately.

Prawn and Dill Bisque

*Good fish soups are curiously rare in Britain,
this one is particularly pleasing.
A bisque was originally the name of a rich
shellfish soup (usually lobster)
from France, but is now used for fish and
shellfish soups.*

S E R V E S 4

450 g / 1 lb cooked whole prawns
(in their shells)

150 ml / 5 fl oz dry white wine

the white part of a slim leek, washed and
shredded

stick of celery, chopped

bunch of parsley

sprig of dill

45 g / 1½ oz butter

30 g / 1 oz flour

150 ml / 5 fl oz double cream

salt and cayenne pepper

G A R N I S H

4 sprigs of dill

O V E N

160°C 325°F Gas Mark 3
Simmering or Baking Oven

Shell the prawns, set the prawns aside and put the shells in a pan with 600 ml / 1 pint of cold water, the wine, leek, celery, parsley and dill. Bring to the boil, cover and cook in a preheated oven – or over moderate heat – for 20 minutes. Strain the stock through a fine-mesh sieve.

Melt the butter in a pan, stir in the flour and cook for 1 minute but do not let it colour. Then, off the heat, gradually incorporate the stock. Cook, stirring, until thickened. Add the peeled prawns and the cream. Season to taste with salt and cayenne pepper. Bring the soup almost to the boil and serve straight away in bowls, each garnished with a sprig of dill.

~

CREAM OF SAFFRON AND MUSSEL SOUP

A rich and delicious broth that brightens a dull January day. Saffron may be expensive but its golden colour and unique flavour make this a perfect soup for a special occasion.

SERVES 6

300 ml / 10 fl oz milk, warmed
225 g / 8 oz shelled cooked mussels
generous pinch of saffron threads
55 g / 2 oz butter
small onion, chopped
small carrot, chopped
stick celery, chopped
slim clove of garlic, peeled and chopped

1 teaspoon flour
150 ml / 5 fl oz dry white wine
bay leaf
300 ml / 10 fl oz fish stock
300 ml / 10 fl oz double cream
salt and freshly milled pepper
1 teaspoon parsley, finely chopped

GARNISH
raw leek and carrot, finely shredded

OVEN
140°C 275°F Gas Mark 1 Simmering Oven
190°C 375°F Gas Mark 5 Roasting Oven

Pour the warm milk over the mussels and saffron. Cover and place in the preheated oven – at the lower temperature – for 30 minutes.

Melt the butter in a saucepan, stir in the onion, carrot, celery and garlic for 2-3 minutes until softened. Stir in the flour and add the wine and bay leaf. Cover and cook the vegetable stock in the preheated oven – at the higher temperature – for 20 minutes.

Strain the vegetable stock and return to the pan. Using a slotted spoon, remove the mussels from the milk and keep warm. Add the fish stock, the milk from the mussels and the cream. Taste and season accordingly with salt and pepper. Bring the soup almost to the boil, then add the parsley and mussels.

Ladle the soup into hot soup bowls and garnish with a few shreds of leek and carrot.

~

CREAM OF MUSHROOM SOUP
UNDER A CRUST

*For their deeper flavour and
darker colour, use medium-size mushrooms
with open caps.*

SERVES 4-6

340 g / 12 oz mushrooms

100 g / 3½ oz butter

1-2 shallots, finely chopped

1 clove garlic, finely chopped

1 tablespoon lemon juice

600 ml / 1 pint chicken or well-flavoured
vegetable stock

150 ml / 5 fl oz milk

2 teaspoons potato flour or cornflour

150 ml / 5 fl oz double cream

1 teaspoon tarragon leaves, chopped

1 teaspoon parsley, chopped

1 tablespoon Manzanilla sherry

salt and freshly milled pepper

170 g / 6 oz prepared-weight puff pastry

1 egg, separated

OVEN
200°C 400°F Gas Mark 6 Roasting Oven

Wipe the mushrooms with a damp cloth and peel them only if they are discoloured. Remove a thin layer from the base of each stalk and discard. Slice the mushrooms thinly. Melt half the butter in a pan and sauté 1 tablespoon of the mushrooms until soft. Use a slotted spoon to transfer the mushrooms to a plate and set aside for the garnish.

Add the remaining butter to the pan and cook the shallots and garlic until soft. Stir in the remaining mushrooms until they have absorbed the butter and add the lemon juice. Pour in the stock, bring to the boil, cover the pan and cook on the hob or in the oven for 15-20 minutes.

Purée the contents of the pan in a processor or blender, or press through a sieve, and return to the pan. Blend the milk with the flour, add to the soup and cook, stirring, until thickened.

Add the cream, tarragon, parsley, sherry, and salt and pepper to taste. Pour the soup into individual ovenproof bowls or one large ovenproof tureen, making sure that the dishes are no more than three-quarters full. Add the reserved mushrooms to the soup. Roll out the pastry and cut a lid for each of the dishes. Brush the rim of each dish with egg white and cover with the pastry lid, pressing the edges down well. Crimp the edge of the pastry, brush with egg yolk and cut 2 or 3 vents in the centre to allow steam to escape.

Place the soup dishes on a baking sheet and bake in the oven for 15-20 minutes until the pastry is golden brown and well puffed up. Serve straight from the oven.

∼

Right
CREAM OF MUSHROOM SOUP
UNDER A CRUST

Sorrel Soup
WITH A SHERRY *SABAYON*

*When David Nichols – now head chef
at The Ritz – prepared my recipe for chilled
sorrel soup for a party he gave it a
marvellous lift by adding a top layer of warm
sherry sabayon. The contrast between
the two temperatures in the soup is a delight.*

SERVES 4-6

115 g / 4 oz sorrel leaves

sprig of tarragon

1 large cucumber, peeled and chopped

1 clove garlic, peeled

1 litre / 1¾ pints jellied chicken stock

150 ml / 5 fl oz double cream

salt

dash of Tabasco sauce

SABAYON

2 tablespoons fino sherry

4 egg yolks

1 teaspoon caster sugar

1 tablespoon jellied chicken stock, warmed

1 tablespoon double cream

GARNISH

4-6 sprigs of chervil

Strip the stems from the sorrel leaves and discard. Wash and drain the leaves and chop roughly. Place in a pan with the tarragon, cucumber, the clove of garlic and the stock. Bring to the boil then cook steadily over moderate heat until soft.

Remove from the heat and purée until smooth in a processor or press through a fine sieve. Chill the soup, then whisk in the cream and season to taste with salt and just a spot of Tabasco sauce. Pour the soup into 4-6 chilled heatproof bowls and keep cold.

Make the *sabayon* by whisking – with a hand-held electric beater – the sherry with the egg yolks and sugar in a porcelain or stainless steel bain-marie (a bowl set over a pan of simmering water) over medium heat for 5-10 minutes until thick and frothy. Remove from the heat and gradually whisk in the jellied stock (made by boiling stock fast over a high heat to reduce) and the cream.

Carefully ladle the *sabayon* on top of the chilled soup and garnish each bowl with chervil. Serve straight away with ALMOND AND CHIVE SABLE BISCUITS (see p115).

Pumpkin and Rosemary Soup

*If you start with a smallish pumpkin, the
flesh can be scooped out to make the
soup, the seeds can be peeled and toasted
to serve with drinks, and the shell can be
used as a tureen – complete with lid.*

SERVES 6

55 g / 2 oz butter

2 shallots, finely chopped

900 g / 2 lb pumpkin flesh, roughly chopped

sprig of fresh rosemary

5 cm / 2 in stick cinnamon

1 litre / 1¾ pints chicken stock

150 ml / 5 fl oz double cream

salt and freshly milled pepper

OVEN

190°C 375°F Gas Mark 5 Roasting Oven

Melt the butter in a saucepan and soften the shallots over medium heat for 5-8 minutes not allowing them to brown at all. Stir in the chopped pumpkin until coated with butter. Add the rosemary and cinnamon, cover the pan and cook for 15 minutes on the hob or in the oven until the pumpkin has yielded some of its liquid. Pour over the stock and bring back to the boil. Cook, covered, on the hob or in the oven for a further 20-30 minutes until the pumpkin is soft.

Discard the rosemary and cinnamon and purée the contents of the pan in a processor or blender. Return the soup to the pan and stir in the cream, season to taste and bring almost to the boil.

Meanwhile place the pumpkin shell on a baking tray in the oven for 5-10 minutes until hot. Transfer to a serving dish, pour in the hot soup and cover with the pumpkin lid and serve.

~

CAULIFLOWER, GINGER AND CORIANDER SOUP

*Indian spices and fresh coriander transform
the flavour of familiar brassicas
such as cauliflower to produce an unusual
and appetizing soup.*

SERVES 4

450 g / 1 lb cauliflower

15 g / ½ oz butter

30 g / 1 oz fresh ginger, peeled and finely chopped

1-2 cloves garlic, peeled and finely chopped

2 cardamom pods, seeds only

1 teaspoon coriander seeds, ground in a mortar and sieved to remove the husks

900 ml / 1½ pints well-flavoured vegetable stock

½ teaspoon salt

1 tablespoon coriander leaves, chopped

80 ml / 3 fl oz *crème fraîche* or double cream

juice of ½ lemon or lime

GARNISH

4 tablespoons set yoghurt and fine threads of lime or lemon zest

HOB OR OVEN

180°C 350°F Gas Mark 4 Roasting Oven

Remove any leaves and the stalk of the cauliflower (if sparkling fresh I add these to a vegetable stock-pot or – finely shredded – to a stir-fry dish) and separate the florets. Melt the butter in a saucepan and cook the ginger and garlic for 2-3 minutes until softened but not coloured. Stir in the cauliflower florets, cardamom seeds and ground coriander for 2 minutes until coated with butter. Add the stock and salt and bring to the boil. Cover, and cook on the hob or in the oven for 15-25 minutes or until the cauliflower is cooked.

Purée the contents of the pan in a blender or processor or press through a fine sieve. Return to the pan and stir in the chopped coriander and the *crème fraîche* or cream. Adjust the flavour with a squeeze of lemon or lime juice which helps to emphasise the ginger in the soup.

Bring almost to boiling then serve in warmed soup bowls. Garnish each bowl with a spoonful of yoghurt and sprinkle with the shredded zest of a lime or lemon.

~

BUTTERMILK BANNOCK
WITH FRESH HERBS

*This Irish soda bread is quick to make and
has an excellent flavour.*

SERVES 4

225 g / 8 oz wholemeal flour

½ teaspoon bicarbonate of soda

1 teaspoon of salt

1 teaspoon mixed chopped fresh thyme
and chives

150 ml / 5 fl oz buttermilk
or plain natural yoghurt

OVEN
220°C 425°F Gas Mark 7 Roasting Oven

If using a terracotta tile as a bake stone, soak
in cold water while you prepare the dough.

Sift the flour, bicarbonate of soda and salt
into a bowl, then add the bran left in the
sieve. Stir the herbs into the buttermilk and
add to the dry ingredients with 1-2 tablespoons of warm water to make a soft dough.
Shape the dough into a round and place on
the (dry) bread stone or on a floured baking
sheet. Mark the top into quarters with a
sharp knife. Place a cake tin over the loaf to
maintain a moist atmosphere around the loaf
during baking.

Bake the loaf in the preheated oven for 30
minutes, remove the cake tin and bake for a
further 10 minutes until the crust is brown.
Remove the loaf from the oven and wrap in
a cloth to keep it warm and place in a basket
for serving.

OVEN-ROAST ASPARAGUS

*An admirable way of cooking
freshly-cut asparagus which I first came
across in Seville. I like the addition
of Gruyère cheese though the dish is equally
good served plain.*

SERVES 4

550 g / 1¼ lb very fresh green asparagus or
450 g / 1lb green asparagus tips

55 g / 2 oz slightly salted butter

2 tablespoons extra virgin olive oil, ideally
Spanish

30-55 g / 1-2 oz Gruyère cheese, thinly shaved
(optional)

OVEN
190°C 375°F Gas Mark 5 Roasting Oven

Trim the ends of the whole asparagus and
cut the stalks to roughly equal lengths.
Asparagus tips should be usable as they are.
Melt the butter with the oil in a large cast-
iron skillet or frying-pan. Add the asparagus
and turn over until evenly coated with butter.
Bake in the preheated oven for 8-15 minutes
or until just cooked.

Divide the asparagus between 4 hot *gratin*
dishes and arrange the shaved cheese across
the centre of the stalks. Replace in the oven
or place under a hot grill until the cheese has
melted. Serve straight away with fresh bread
to mop up the buttery juices.

Right
OVEN-ROAST ASPARAGUS

TOMATO, TARRAGON AND ORANGE SORBET

On a summer's day that's warm enough for lunch in the garden, this attractive sorbet, served in orange skin shells makes an appealing first course.

S E R V E S 6

450 g / 1lb ripe, full-flavoured tomatoes

1 slim clove garlic, peeled

1 bay leaf

15 cm / 6 in strip of zest of orange

1 teaspoon sugar

¼ teaspoon salt

8 tarragon leaves, finely chopped

6 medium-sized sweet oranges, preferably seedless Navels

1-2 tablespoons of Chablis

G A R N I S H

sprigs of mint, or citrus or bay leaves

O V E N
160°C 325°F Gas Mark 3 Simmering Oven

Wash and dry the tomatoes, quarter them and put in a saucepan or casserole with the garlic, bay leaf, zest of orange, sugar and salt. Bring to the boil, cover and cook in a pre-heated oven for 20-30 minutes until the tomatoes are cooked. Try not to overcook or the lovely fresh taste of tomatoes is lost. Pour the contents of the pan into a fine sieve and press through, leaving the tomato skins and seeds, garlic, bay leaf and zest of orange which are to be discarded. While the mixture is still warm stir in the tarragon.

Wash and dry the oranges. Cut a lid from the side opposite the stalk of each orange

and reserve. Taking care not to break the orange skin shells, scoop the flesh – discarding any pips – into a processor and whizz to a purée. Strain through a sieve into the tomato mixture. Stir in the wine with sugar and salt to taste. Freeze the mixture in a sorbetière or in a bowl in the freezer until firm.

Meanwhile chill or freeze the orange shells and their lids. Spoon the sorbet into each orange shell, heaping it a little above the rim. Replace the orange lids at an angle. Serve immediately, garnished with sprigs of mint or an orange leaf.

SUMMER HERB CUSTARDS

A delicate first course that depends for its fine flavour on a handful of freshly picked herbs.

S E R V E S 4

small knob of butter

small handful of mixed fresh herbs – choose 2 or 3 from parsley, tarragon, chives, basil, bay and thyme

300 ml / 10 fl oz whole milk

sliver of garlic

1 egg

2 egg yolks

salt and milled green peppercorns

O V E N
190°C 375°F Gas Mark 5 Roasting Oven

Butter 4 small cocotte dishes and place a disc of non-stick paper in each base.

Roughly chop the herbs and place in a small, heavy-based pan with the milk and the garlic. Slowly warm the milk and place over low heat for 15 minutes. Stir now and again with a wooden spoon, pressing the herbs to release their flavour. Raise the heat and bring almost to the boil. Remove from the heat, leave to infuse for 5 minutes then strain into a jug.

Lightly whisk the egg with the yolks, then stir into the herb-flavoured milk. Season with salt and milled pepper. Strain the mixture into the cocotte dishes and place in a bain-marie or a roasting pan of warm water.

Bake in the preheated oven for 20-25 minutes, until the custards are set in the centre. Allow to rest for 2 minutes then loosen the edge of each custard with a knife blade and turn out on to warm plates. Serve with HERB BUTTER (see page 32) or a warm fresh tomato sauce.

~

GERMAN ONION TART

This is the Nahe Valley version of this famous German speciality, made by a friend in the tiny village of Winterburg to accompany jugs of federweisser, *the cloudy, yeast-rich liquid from the first pressing of grapes.*

SERVES 6

RICH SHORTCRUST PASTRY
170 g / 6 oz plain flour
100 g / 3½ oz butter
1 egg yolk mixed with 2 tablespoons cold water
FILLING
680 g / 1½ lb onions
55 g / 2 oz butter

1 tablespoon mild olive oil
2 eggs
2 egg yolks
150 ml / 5 fl oz single cream
freshly grated nutmeg or 1 teaspoon caraway seeds
salt and freshly milled black pepper

OVEN
200°C 400°F Gas Mark 6
Roasting or Baking Oven
160°C 325°F Gas Mark 3 Simmering Oven
180°C 350°F Gas Mark 4
Roasting or Baking Oven

Make the pastry and set aside in a cool place for 30 minutes. Roll out the pastry and line a buttered 23cm/9in diameter fluted tart tin. Cover the base with a circle of non-stick baking paper and baking beans. Bake in a preheated oven (first temperature) for 10 minutes. Remove the paper and beans and bake for a further 5 minutes. Turn oven down.

Meanwhile peel and slice the onions very finely. Melt the butter with the oil in a heavy-based casserole. Add the onions and cook, covered, in a low or Simmering Oven (second temperature) for 30 minutes until they are soft and golden. Remove from the oven and allow to cool.

Beat the eggs, egg yolks and cream together lightly with a fork. Season with plenty of nutmeg or the caraway seeds and some salt and pepper. Pour on to the onions and spoon the mixture into the tart case.

Bake on a baking sheet in an oven preheated to the third temperature above for 25-30 minutes or until the filling is set in the centre. Serve straight away.

~

FOCACCIA
WITH ANCHOIADE AND ESCABECHE OLIVES

Italian flat bread, rich with olive oil and sage or rosemary is very easy to make at home. Focaccia is particularly good served warm with an anchovy and garlic dressing and a simple Mediterranean meal. In the country I depend upon dried yeast since it keeps well, tightly covered, in the fridge for at least a month.

MAKES ONE LOAF

1 teaspoon dried yeast granules such as Allinsons

450 ml / ¾ pint lukewarm water

1 teaspoon white sugar (optional)

2 teaspoons sea salt

800 g / 1¾ lb white unbleached bread flour

6-8 tablespoons olive oil

2-3 teaspoons rosemary or sage leaves, finely chopped

few extra leaves to decorate the bread

sea salt crystals

OVEN
190°C 375°F Gas Mark 5 Roasting Oven

Measure the yeast into a warmed mixing bowl. Stir in one-third of the water and if the kitchen is very cold stir in the sugar. (The sugar is not strictly necessary but if you are concerned that the yeast will be reluctant to work due to its age or the low temperature of the kitchen then add it.) Leave in a warm place for about 10 minutes until the surface is foamy. Meanwhile stir the salt into the flour and leave in a warm place.

When the yeast is frothy add the flour and salt, half the olive oil, the chopped herbs and most of the remaining water. Mix until you have a soft dough, adding more water as necessary. Don't make the dough too wet or too dry. Turn the dough on to a floured board and knead for 5-8 minutes until it feels elastic and the surface feels cool and satiny. Return it to the bowl, cover with a cloth or a wooden board and leave in a warm place for about 1 hour or until doubled in volume.

Turn the dough on to a floured board and knead for 1 minute. Shape into a large flat circle or rectangle. Place on an oiled baking sheet or in a roasting tin and brush some of the remaining oil over the top. Leave in a warm place to rise again for 20-30 minutes or until doubled in thickness. Make a series of indentations over the surface of the loaf by pressing the top with your fingertip in 10-15 places. Bake in the preheated oven (on the floor of the Roasting Oven) for 25-35 minutes until golden brown on top and well baked.

Transfer to a wire rack and dribble the remaining olive oil over the top of the loaf so that the oil collects in the depressions. Sprinkle with sea salt crystals and serve while still warm, accompanied by a bowl of the dipping sauce ANCHOIADE (see p55) and a dish of ESCABECHE-STYLE OLIVES (see over the page).

Left

FOCACCIA WITH ANCHOIADE AND ESCABECHE OLIVES *page 26*

∼

ESCABECHE-STYLE OLIVES

Escabeche is a Spanish technique in which food is marinated and pickled in a spicy mixture.

225 g / 8 oz green olives
½ lemon, thinly sliced
1 clove garlic, peeled and sliced
½ (or more according to taste) red chilli pepper, finely chopped
½ teaspoon coriander seeds, bruised
2 teaspoons tomato paste

If the olives are in brine, drain well and tip into a bowl. Quarter the slices of lemon and add to the bowl with the garlic, chopped chilli pepper, coriander seeds and tomato paste. Mix everything together and spoon into a jar. Cover and keep in a cold place or the refrigerator for at least 3 days before serving – try to turn the jar every day to release the flavours.

≈

TOMATO TARTS WITH HERB BUTTER

With their pleasing contrast of textures, these buttery tomato tarts make an excellent first course to a light summer meal.

SERVES 6

255 g / 9 oz prepared-weight puff pastry
85 g / 3 oz unsalted butter, softened
2 tablespoons finely chopped fresh herbs: basil, parsley and chives

a little finely grated lemon zest
squeeze of lemon juice
3 large marmande or beefsteak tomatoes
salt and freshly milled black pepper

OVEN
200°C 400°F Gas Mark 6 Roasting Oven

Divide the pastry into 6 pieces. On a floured board roll out each piece to make a 15 cm / 6 in round.

Blend the butter with the herbs, lemon zest and juice until well combined. Spread two-thirds of the herb butter over each round of pastry and place on a baking sheet, lined with baking paper or non-stick linen.

Slice the tomatoes very thinly and place 3-4 slices, slightly overlapping, on each pastry round. Dot the remaining herb butter over the tomato slices. Season with salt and pepper.

Bake in the preheated oven for 15-20 minutes until the pastry is crisp and golden. The tomatoes will be cooked to perfection and the herbs and lemon will have infused the melted butter. Serve straight away.

≈

Right
TOMATO TARTS WITH HERB BUTTER

SWEDISH JANSON'S TEMPTATION

For the authentic flavour look for Swedish tinned anchovies which are larger and meatier than the Mediterranean kind.

SERVES 2-4

30 g / 1 oz butter
300 g / 10 oz waxy potatoes, peeled
1 small onion, finely chopped
55 g / 2 oz anchovy fillets, in oil
salt
150 ml / 5 fl oz double cream

OVEN
200°C 400°F Gas Mark 6 Roasting Oven

Rub half the butter over the inside of 2 or 4 *gratin* dishes. Finely grate the potatoes and divide half between the *gratin* dishes. Sprinkle over half the onion and place the drained anchovy fillets on top. Add the remaining onion and cover with the rest of the grated potato. Season lightly with salt – the anchovies are already salty. Reserve 2 tablespoons of cream and divide the rest between the dishes spooning it over the potato. Dot with the remaining butter.

Bake in the preheated oven for 25-30 minutes or until the potato is cooked. Spoon over the remaining cream and serve straight away. Follow with a crisp green salad.

～

Left
SCALLOPS IN LIME BUTTER

SCALLOPS IN LIME BUTTER

For their superior flavour and texture, use fresh rather than frozen scallops.

SERVES 4

8 scallops with their coral
salt
1 lime, zest and juice
½ teaspoon pink peppercorns, lightly crushed
55 g / 2 oz butter
4 sheets filo pastry
GARNISH
1-2 handfuls of young salad leaves dressed with hazelnut oil vinaigrette

OVEN
200°C 400°F Gas Mark 6
Roasting or Baking Oven

Rinse and dry the scallops. If necessary, remove the black thread of the intestine. Detach the corals and cut the white part of each scallop into two or three slices. Season the corals and scallops lightly with salt.

Place the lime zest in a small pan with the pink peppercorns and the butter. Melt over a low heat. Sprinkle lime juice over the scallops.

Cut each sheet of filo pastry into 2 squares. Brush with melted butter. Place one square on the other to make an 8-point star. Divide the scallops between the pastry stars and spoon the lime butter over them. Gather the pastry points and pinch to make a parcel.

Bake on a non-stick baking sheet in a preheated oven for 10-12 minutes until the pastry is crisp and golden. Serve immediately, garnished with the young leaves.

～

CROUSTADES OF PRAWNS
IN WHISKY

*Buttery croustades can be made
ahead and stored in the freezer to be filled
with a savoury mixture at a
moment's notice. Serve as a first course
or as light lunch or supper dish.*

SERVES 3 - 6

45 g / 1½ oz butter, melted

6 slices medium thickness bread, white or
wholemeal

FILLING

1 shallot, finely chopped

30 g / 1 oz butter

2 tablespoons whisky

225 g / 8 oz shelled, cooked prawns

4 tablespoons double cream

¼ teaspoon finely chopped fresh young
rosemary leaves

salt and freshly milled black pepper

55 g / 2 oz Gruyère cheese, grated

GARNISH

few rocket leaves or sprigs of watercress

OVEN

200°C 400°F Gas Mark 6 Roasting Oven

To make the croustades, brush 6 tartlet or
patty tins with melted butter. Use a cookie
cutter to cut a circle from each slice of bread.
Press the circles of bread into the tartlet tins
as if lining them with pastry. Brush each
croustade with the rest of the butter and
bake in a preheated oven for 15-20 minutes
until golden and crisp. If making ahead, cool
the croustades and store in a cold place or
the freezer until needed.

Make the filling by softening the shallot in
the butter in a pan over medium heat for 3-5
minutes, not allowing it to change colour.
Turn up the heat, add the whisky and allow
to bubble for a minute. The alcohol will be
boiled off, leaving the unique taste of
whisky. Lower the heat, stir in the prawns,
cream and chopped rosemary. Fresh rosemary is more subtle in flavour than the dried
form. Bring almost to boiling point, season to
taste and spoon into the warm croustades.
Sprinkle the Gruyère cheese on top and
place under a hot grill or back in the oven
for a few minutes until the cheese has melted
and is brown. Run a knife round the edge of
each croustade and carefully lift them out of
the tartlet tins. Serve straight away garnished
with a few rocket or watercress leaves.

~

Right

CROUSTADES OF PRAWNS
IN WHISKY

Potato *Latkes*
with Smoked Salmon and
Soured Cream

Fried pancakes of grated potato are common to the traditional cooking of several European countries. For Swiss rosti, *the potatoes should be parboiled before grating, Polish* latkes *are prepared with raw grated potato and some finely chopped onion, if you wish – our family favourite for Christmas Eve lunch in the kitchen.*

SERVES 4-8

450 g / 1lb peeled waxy potatoes, like Desirée

1 clove garlic, peeled and crushed with a good pinch of salt

grapeseed oil for shallow frying

170-225 g / 6-8 oz smoked salmon

150 ml / 5 fl oz soured cream or *crème fraîche*

freshly milled black pepper

1 lemon, quartered

GARNISH

8 sprigs of fresh dill

OVEN

200°C 400°F Gas Mark 6 Roasting Oven

Grate the potatoes into a bowl – or use the grating attachment on a food processor. Mix in the garlic and salt and divide into 8 small heaps. Heat a thin layer of oil in a cast-iron skillet or frying-pan and drop the ragged heaps into the pan. Use the prongs of a fork to gently flatten them to make *latkes* (thin potato pancakes), about the diameter of a cricket ball. Fry for 3 minutes until the underside is golden brown. Turn them over and fry for 2-3 minutes then transfer to a baking tray in the preheated oven for 5 minutes to cook right through.

Cut the smoked salmon into 8 pieces. Transfer the *latkes* to kitchen paper to remove any surplus fat, then place on 4-8 warm plates. Cover each potato pancake with a piece of smoked salmon, season with black pepper and a little lemon juice and top with a spoonful of soured cream garnished with a sprig of dill. Serve straight away.

Duck Liver Parfait

If duck livers are unavailable, this very rich mousse with a light, creamy texture is almost as delicious made with chicken livers. Serve the mousse warm with a smooth herb butter sauce.

SERVES 6

225 g / 8 oz duck livers

4 eggs, size 3

4 egg yolks

sliver of garlic, crushed

¼ teaspoon dried thyme, finely ground

300 ml / 10 fl oz single cream

150 ml / 5 fl oz milk

salt and freshly milled pepper

knob of butter

HERB BUTTER

15 g / ½ oz parsley leaves

15 g / ½ oz chervil leaves

2 tablespoons finely chopped chives

30 g / 1 oz watercress or land cress

100 g / 3½ oz unsalted butter, melted
a dash of tarragon vinegar or lemon juice
salt and freshly milled pepper

GARNISH
a few sprigs of chervil

OVEN
160°C 325°F Gas Mark 3
Simmering or Baking Oven

Chop the livers finely in a food processor. Mix in the eggs, egg yolks, garlic, thyme, cream and milk. Press the mixture through a fine sieve into a jug and season lightly with salt and pepper.

Butter 6 small moulds or ramekin dishes and place a circle of buttered greaseproof paper in the base of each. Pour the mixture into the moulds and stand them on a layer of folded newspaper in a bain-marie with warm water deep enough to come halfway up the moulds or ramekins.

Cook in the preheated oven for 20-30 minutes or until set. Take care not to overcook the mousses or the texture may be spoiled. The mousse is set when the blade of a knife comes out clean from the centre.

To make the herb butter, rinse the herbs and watercress in cold water and cook in the water clinging to the leaves for 3-4 minutes until softened but still bright green. Purée in a processor or blender, with a little water if necessary, until smooth. Add the melted butter in a trickle, adjust the flavour with tarragon vinegar or lemon juice. Season lightly with salt and pepper and spoon into a warm jug or dish.

To serve, run the blade of a knife round each mousse and turn out on to a small plate. Remove the paper, spoon a little herb butter on top and decorate with a sprig or two of chervil.

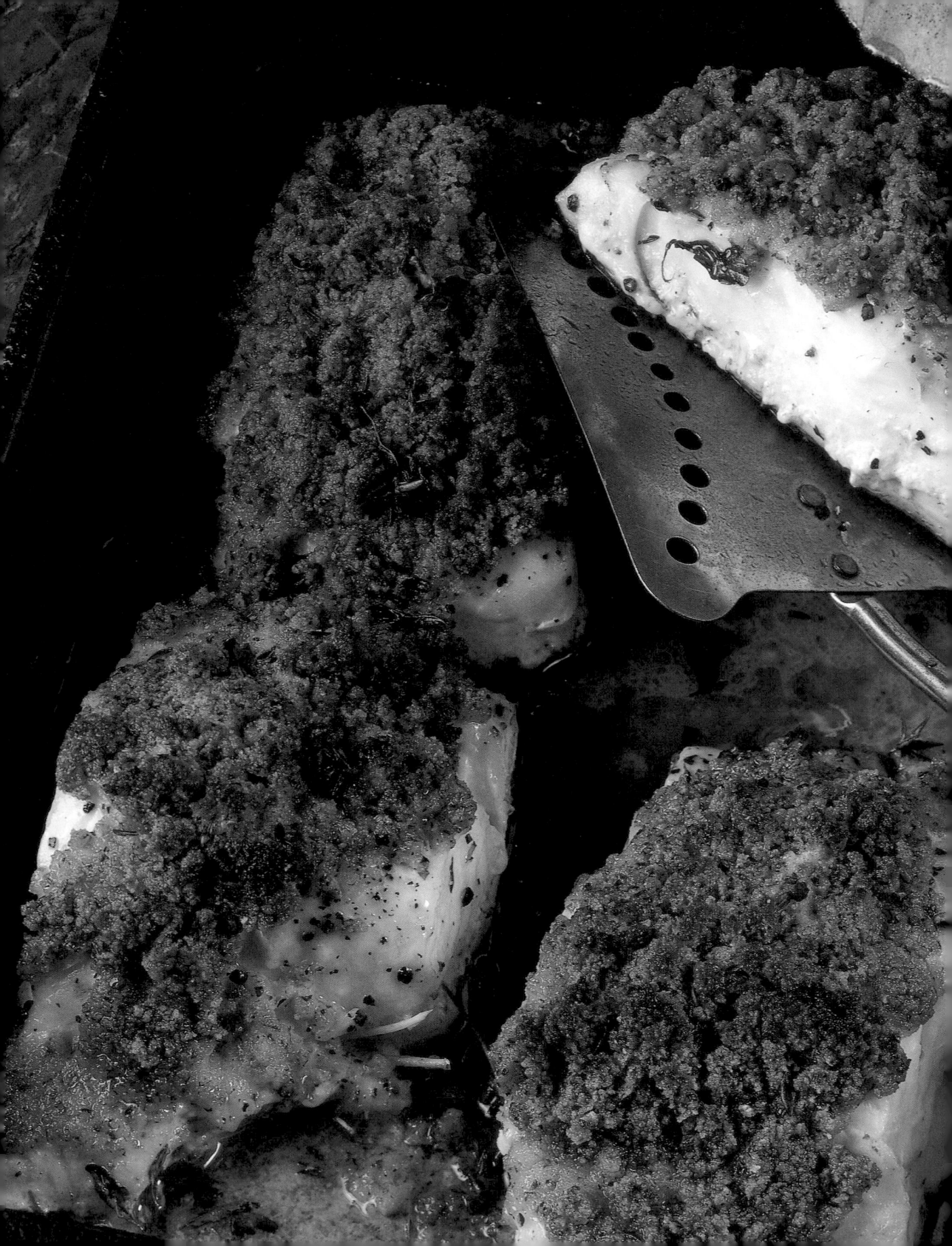

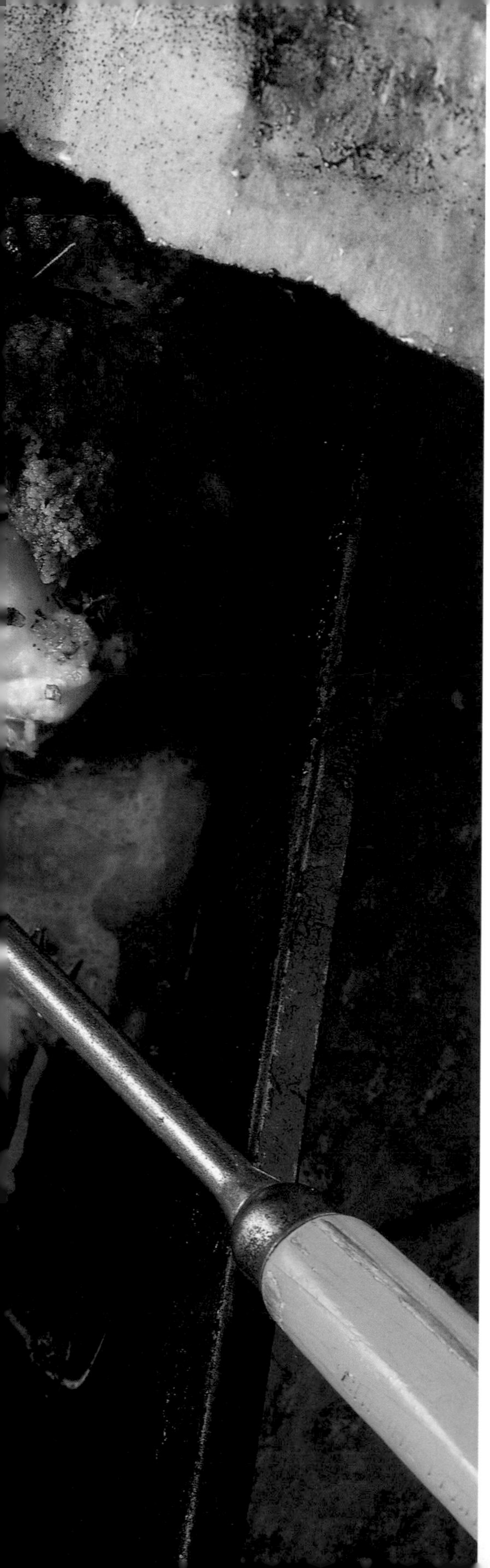

CHAPTER 2

FISH AND SHELLFISH

Now that sparkling fresh fish can arrive in our kitchens almost every day of the year - if need be by overnight courier straight from the port - we are able to enjoy the most delicious fish cookery ever devised.

Left
COD ROASTED WITH A HERB CRUST
page 43

FISH NO longer needs to be overcooked and drenched in strong-tasting sauces, in order to conceal its questionable age. At last, we can all indulge in the remarkable flavour of really fresh fish.

The kitchen pun about keeping a fish out of water is sound advice. For it is folly to waste the flavour of this fine food by diluting it in too much water or stock. But, just as important as the cooking medium, is the cooking method. This is why cooking fish in a traditional oven is my preferred way of preparing this delicate ingredient. The application of heat from all directions – rather than from only one side, as on the hob, means that fish baked in an oven is cooked more quickly and with the minimum loss of moisture and flavour.

What could be simpler than to arrange a fillet of sole or brill, or a cutlet of halibut or salmon – or even whole small fish like a dab or a plaice – in a buttered oven dish. Season lightly and add a splash of lemon juice, cream or wine, sprinkle with chopped parsley or chives, and bake in a hot oven for a matter of minutes. In the oven, the cooking liquid combines with the juices from the fish to produce its own superb sauce. Another oven-cooking method that I use a great deal was much favoured by the Victorians. This is

to cook fish in a paper bag – or if you prefer, a foil envelope – so that it steams in its own liquid. You can cook both a whole salmon or the smallest *goujons* of sole in this way, which is known in the French kitchen as cooking *en papillote*. Even a largish leaf, possibly of lettuce, spinach, or Chinese cabbage – briefly blanched to make it a little more pliable – wrapped around fish to be cooked in the oven acts as an effective and edible green envelope.

It's worth remembering that cooking fish is similar to setting an egg. Indeed, both foods – when free-range and perfectly fresh – are edible when raw, we cook them simply to alter their texture and flavour. Fish is cooked once the flesh is opaque and is coming free from the bone. A general guide to its cooking time in a hot oven is to allow 8-10 minutes per 2.5 cm/1 in thickness of fish. Simply adjust the cooking time according to the nature and cut of your fish. However, oven-cooked fish should be removed from the oven just slightly underdone, because the heat of the dish continues the cooking process as you carry the fish to the table. Perfectly cooked fish and shellfish requires judgement in the kitchen, yet nothing rewards the skilful cook quite so vividly as the revelation of flavour that results from taking care with this noble wild food.

BAKED SALMON
WITH SORREL CREAM SAUCE

*A whole salmon or salmon trout, prepared
this way with the slightly aniseed
flavour of herb fennel, makes a fine centre-
piece for a buffet lunch or supper party.*

SERVES 6 - 8

1.5 kg / 3½ lb salmon or salmon trout, cleaned
and ready to cook

salt

3-4 handfuls of 15 cm / 6 in shoots of herb fennel

150 ml / 5 fl oz dry white wine

SORREL CREAM SAUCE

100 g / 3½ oz sorrel leaves

½ teaspoon finely grated zest of lemon

sliver of garlic, crushed

300 ml / 10 fl oz double cream

salt and freshly milled black pepper

juice of ½ lemon

dash of balsamic or sherry vinegar

GARNISH

sprigs of fennel

OVEN

190°C 375°F Gas Mark 5 Roasting Oven

Cover a large oven tray or roasting tin with a double thickness of cooking foil large enough to enclose the fish. Season the inside of the fish with a little salt and tuck in some of the fennel. Make a bed of fennel on the foil and place the fish on it. Cover the fish with more fennel and pour over the wine.

Fold up the foil to enclose the fish and secure the edges firmly.

Bake in the preheated oven for 25-30 minutes depending on the size. The fish is cooked as soon as the flesh is opaque but remember that it continues to cook a little as it cools. Remove from the oven and set aside for 10 minutes.

Unwrap the fish, carefully transfer to a large serving dish and discard the cooked fennel. Make a neat cut through the skin in a curved line behind the head. Gently pull off the skin, in sections if that is easier, removing the gills but leaving the tail intact. If necessary, scrape away the grey fatty layer to reveal the pink flesh. Decorate the fish and the dish with the extra sprigs of fresh fennel, and serve warm or set aside until cold.

You can make the sorrel cream sauce earlier in the day or while the fish is cooking. Strip the stalks from the sorrel leaves, wash leaves in cold water and drain. Cook the wet sorrel leaves in a heavy-based pan over moderate heat until reduced to an olive green purée and all surplus water has been driven off. Remove from the heat and beat the purée until smooth, then mix in the lemon zest and garlic. Whisk the cream until thick but still glossy and fold in the sorrel purée. Season with salt and pepper and add lemon juice and vinegar to taste so that the sauce is just pleasantly sharp. Spoon the sorrel cream into a bowl or jug and serve with the salmon.

Hot Salmon and Dill Creams

Serve this delicate fish mousse, cooked in individual moulds, as either a first or a fish course. A neat way of ensuring the mousse does not stick to the mould during cooking is to line the buttered moulds with young blanched spinach leaves before spooning in the raw mixture.

SERVES 4

200 g / 7 oz fresh salmon, skinned, boned and chilled

1 egg, chilled

150 ml / 5 fl oz double cream, chilled

salt and freshly milled black pepper

½ teaspoon chopped dill

ORANGE GINGER BUTTER

55 g / 2 oz unsalted butter

¼ teaspoon finely grated fresh ginger

½ teaspoon fine shreds of orange zest

1 tablespoon of orange juice

GARNISH

a handful of leaves of rocket and lamb's lettuce

sprigs of dill and some long fine shreds of orange zest

OVEN

180°C 350°F Gas Mark 4 Roasting Oven

Cut the salmon into pieces and place in the bowl of a processor with the egg and 115 ml / 4 fl oz of the cream. Process for 2-3 minutes to make a thick purée. Season lightly with salt and pepper and stir in the dill.

Divide the mixture between 4 well-buttered dariole moulds and smooth level. Cook in a bain-marie, or in a roasting pan with warm water to half the depth of the moulds, in the preheated oven for about 15-20 minutes until set.

Meanwhile melt the butter with the ginger and orange zest and stir over moderate heat to extract the flavour. Stir in the orange juice and keep warm.

Unmould each salmon mousse on to a small plate. Spoon over a little strained butter and garnish with a few leaves and shreds of orange zest. Serve straight away.

Lady Clark's Salmon Cutlets
EN PAPILLOTE

A beautifully simple idea from the classic work on nineteenth century country house cooking, The Cookery Book of Lady Clark of Tillypronie. *The cooking method is useful for other fish such as turbot and halibut, with alternative seasonings such as shredded fresh ginger, coriander and lemon grass.*

SERVES 4

4 salmon cutlets

salt and milled black pepper

1 tablespoon finely chopped chives or mushrooms

1 tablespoon finely chopped parsley

4 tablespoons fino sherry

4 x 25 cm / 10 in square sheets baking paper

OVEN

200°C 400°F Gas Mark 6 Roasting Oven

Pat the salmon cutlets dry with kitchen paper, and season lightly. Mix the chives or mushrooms and parsley together and sprinkle over both sides of the salmon. Place each cutlet in the centre of the sheet of baking paper and spoon the sherry over the fish. Fold up the paper to enclose the salmon, securing it by twisting like a Christmas cracker or use wooden pegs to keep it from unfolding during cooking.

Place the paper parcels on a baking sheet. Cook in the preheated oven for 8-15 minutes, depending on the thickness of the fish, or until the salmon has just turned milky and is parting from the bone. Serve straight away, in their paper wrapping, and accompany with new buttered potatoes or bread.

To serve cold, or at a picnic – allow the salmon cutlets to cool in their paper envelopes, then chill for several hours until the fish juices and sherry have set to a delicious jelly before serving.

SALMON IN A CASE

One of the best English fish pies, first – and now famously – revived by George Perry-Smith at The Hole in the Wall in Bath during the 1950s.

S E R V E S   6 - 8

450 g / 1 lb prepared-weight all-butter puff pastry or flaky pastry
1.5-2 kg / 3½-4¼ lb salmon, cut into 2 skinless fillets
salt and freshly milled black pepper
½ bitter or Seville orange
115 g / 4 oz butter, softened
55 g / 2 oz preserved ginger, chopped
30 g / 1 oz blanched almonds, slivered
30 g / 1 oz currants
1 egg yolk

O v e n

200°C 400°F Gas Mark 6
Roasting or Baking Oven

Divide the pastry in half and roll out each piece on a floured board to roughly the shape of the fish, and about 3 mm / ⅛ in thick. Chill the pastry in a freezer or refrigerator while you prepare the fish.

Season the salmon all over and sprinkle with the juice of the orange. Mix the butter with the finely grated zest of the orange, the preserved ginger, almonds and currants.

Place one sheet of pastry on a baking tray lined with non-stick baking paper. Arrange one fillet of salmon on top and spread over half the butter mixture. Trim the pastry around the fish allowing a 2.5 cm / 1 in margin. Place the other fillet on top to re-form the salmon and spread over the rest of the butter. Cover with the other sheet of pastry. Trim the pastry so that it is slightly larger than the fish, brush the edges with water, press together and tuck under the fish. Brush the pastry case with egg yolk.

Bake in a preheated oven for 30-40 minutes until the pastry is golden. Serve hot, cut into slices, with the BITTER ORANGE AND CHIVE SAUCE (see over), or when cold with mayonnaise spiked with the zest and juice of a Seville orange.

BITTER ORANGE AND CHIVE SAUCE

Each fruit can be replaced with the juice of one sweet orange and half a lemon.

MAKES 300ML/10FL OZ

30 g / 1 oz caster sugar

90 ml / 3 fl oz dry white wine

125 ml / 4½ fl oz Seville orange juice, strained

½ teaspoon finely grated zest of Seville orange

short stick of celery

½ clove garlic, peeled

1 teaspoon potato flour

2-3 tablespoons finely chopped chives

salt and freshly milled green peppercorns

45 g / 1½ oz butter

In a small heavy-based saucepan, dissolve the sugar in 1 tablespoon cold water over a low heat. Raise the heat and cook until the sugar caramelizes to orange-brown. Remove from the heat and carefully add the wine, orange juice and zest, celery and garlic.

Return to the heat and stir until the caramelized sugar is dissolved. Blend the potato flour with 1 tablespoon cold water and stir into the mixture. Cook, stirring, for 5-6 minutes until thickened. Keep hot until just before serving. Discard the celery and garlic and stir in the chives. Season to taste. When almost ready to serve, add the butter in small pieces and stir until melted. Pour the sauce into a warm jug or bowl and serve with SALMON IN A CASE (see p39) or other hot salmon dishes.

MACKEREL POACHED IN TEA

This is an unusual and good, cold fish dish; the recipe comes from the West Country where freshly-caught mackerel are still an inexpensive treat.

SERVES 4

4 medium-sized mackerel, cleaned and ready to cook

sea salt

4 bay leaves

12 black peppercorns

1 tablespoon dark muscovado sugar

85 ml / 3 fl oz cold, black tea – I like smoky-flavoured Lapsang Souchong

85 ml / 3 fl oz cider vinegar

OVEN
180°C 350°F Gas Mark 4
Roasting or Baking Oven

Dry the fish with kitchen paper, season lightly and arrange in an ovenproof dish. Add the bay leaves and peppercorns. Mix the sugar with the tea and the vinegar and pour over the fish. Place a sheet of foil over the fish.

Bake in the preheated oven for 20-30 minutes until the fish are just cooked. Remove from the oven and allow to cool, then chill. Serve when the liquid has set to a light jelly, and the fish have acquired a delicate flavour.

Right
MACKEREL POACHED IN TEA

TORBAY SOLE
STUFFED WITH LIME AND CHIVE BUTTER

*Torbay sole is not seen much beyond Devon,
however either Dover sole or lemon
sole – or even dabs – taste excellent when
cooked this way.
Fillets of fish can simply be spread
with the butter and baked. Other savoury
butters which work well with fish
are tarragon and orange, dill and lemon,
or coriander and fresh ginger.*

SERVES 4

4 Torbay soles
salt
150 g / 5 oz slightly salted butter, softened
juice and finely grated zest of 1 lime
1 tablespoon finely chopped chives
2 tablespoons dry breadcrumbs

OVEN
200°C 400°F Gas Mark 6 Roasting Oven

Clean the fish, remove the heads and dark skin, and use kitchen scissors to cut off the spiky fins that run along each side. Or ask your fishmonger to do this. Then use a sharp knife to make a pocket on each side of the backbone by sliding a knife against the cross bones to free the flesh. Lightly salt the fish all over and place in a well buttered ovenproof dish – or in 4 individual *gratin* dishes.

Melt 30 g / 1 oz of the butter in a small pan and set aside. Cream the remaining butter with the juice and half the finely grated zest of lime. Mix in the chives. Divide the butter

between the fish, spreading it into the pockets as far as you can. Brush the melted butter over the fish, mix the breadcrumbs with the remaining grated zest and sprinkle on top.

Bake the fish in the preheated oven for 20-30 minutes or until the fish is cooked right through. Serve straight away.

ELIZA ACTON'S
SOLE
BAKED IN CREAM

*In her recipe for 'Soles Stewed in Cream',
Eliza Acton observes, 'In Cornwall
the fish is laid at once into thick clotted
cream, and stewed entirely in
it'. She writes that she prefers the flavour
of the dish when the fish is first
poached in water for 2 minutes. Having tried
both methods, I find that provided
your fish is sparkling fresh, the simple
Cornish way is very good indeed.*

SERVES 1

1 medium-large fillet of sole or brill
salt
ground mace
cayenne pepper
½ lemon
3-4 tablespoons double cream
1 teaspoon finely chopped parsley or chives
(optional)

OVEN
200°C 400°F Gas Mark 6 Roasting Oven

Pat the fish dry with kitchen paper and season lightly with salt, mace and cayenne pepper. Squeeze a little lemon juice over both sides of the fish and place in a shallow oven dish. Spoon the cream over the fish and, if you wish, sprinkle the herbs on top – although these do not appear in Miss Acton's original recipe.

Bake in the preheated oven for 8-10 minutes or until the flesh of the fish is opaque and just cooked. Serve straight away.

∽

COD
ROASTED WITH A
HERB CRUST

*Other richly flavoured fish such as halibut
and salmon can be cooked this way,
protected from the fierce heat of the oven by
the herb-rich crust.
Although, for speed, I usually prepare
the crust in a processor, the chopping and
mixing can be done equally well
by hand if you prefer.*

SERVES 4

4 x 170g/6oz pieces of cod fillet, as thick as
possible
juice of 1 lemon
salt and freshly milled pepper
knob of butter
115g/4oz fresh white bread, crusts removed
½ teacup chopped fresh summer herbs, such as
parsley, chervil, chives, coriander, basil,
tarragon, mint

½ teaspoon finely grated lemon zest
55g/2oz butter, melted
2 tablespoons medium dry white wine

OVEN
200°C 400°F Gas Mark 6 Roasting Oven

Pat the fish dry with kitchen paper, then sprinkle with half the lemon juice, and season lightly with salt and pepper. Place the fish in one large or four individual well-buttered oven dishes.

Break the bread into the bowl of a processor, add the herbs and blend until the bread has formed crumbs and the mixture is pale green. Add the lemon zest, some salt and pepper, and two-thirds of the butter with the remaining lemon juice. Process again until the mixture lightly binds together – if necessary add a sprinkling of cold water to achieve this.

Spoon the herb crust over the fish, lightly pressing it down in an even layer. Pour over the remaining butter, spoon the wine around the fish and cover with buttered paper.

Bake in the preheated oven for 20-25 minutes or until the fish is cooked and just opaque. Serve straight away, with minted new potatoes.

∽

Monkfish *Brochettes*
WITH BAY LEAVES

If you have access to a mature herb garden, the young branches of bay or rosemary make charming and aromatic brochettes *or skewers for cooking the marinated fish, otherwise wooden skewers soaked for half an hour in cold water work perfectly well.*

SERVES 4

680-900 g / 1½-2 lb skinned monkfish tail

1 lemon

1-2 tablespoons clear local honey

2 tablespoons olive oil

1 tablespoon chopped mint leaves

salt and freshly milled green or black peppercorns

2 yellow sweet peppers

24-30 stoned black olives (optional)

8-12 fresh bay leaves

a little extra olive oil

8 freshly-made *brochettes* or presoaked wooden skewers

Carefully inspect the fish for any errant bones and remove. Cut the fish into 30-40 even-sized pieces.

Wash and dry the lemon, then use a zester to remove the thin aromatic part of the lemon skin in long fine shreds. Place in a wide shallow dish and add the strained juice of the lemon, honey, olive oil and mint. Stir, then check the taste and season lightly with salt and pepper. Add the fish and turn over in the marinade until evenly coated. Set aside in a cool place for 30-60 minutes for the fish to absorb the flavours.

Remove the core and seeds of the sweet peppers and cut into pieces about the same size as the fish. Put in a shallow bowl with the olives and bay leaves and drizzle over a little olive oil.

Thread the fish, peppers, olives and bay leaves on to the *brochettes* or wooden skewers. Heat a cast-iron griddle pan on the hob until very hot. Place the *brochettes* in the pan and allow to colour slightly in several places. Transfer the griddle pan to the oven, and cook in the hottest place for 6-12 minutes or until the fish is just cooked and pearly white. Serve straight away with crusty bread or BROWN RICE WITH INDIAN SPICED CASHEW NUTS (see p58).

Right
MONKFISH *BROCHETTES*
WITH BAY LEAVES

Mussels
with almond and
coriander butter

*A small one-woman restaurant in Arles
produced mussels with almond butter
one Sunday evening some years ago. It's such
a good combination that I cook it often,
sometimes with fresh coriander, otherwise
with chives or tarragon.*

S E R V E S   4

450 g / 1 lb or 2 pints fresh mussels

150 ml / 5 fl oz dry white wine

1 shallot, finely chopped

few stalks of parsley

bay leaf

70 g / 2½ oz whole blanched almonds

70 g / 2½ oz butter, softened

squeeze of lemon juice

1 tablespoon coriander leaves, chopped

O V E N
200°C 400°F Gas Mark 6 Roasting Oven

Scrub the mussels under cold running water and remove the 'beard' of fine threads. Discard any mussels that will not close completely when tapped, and any that are unusually heavy – they may contain sand or mud. Drain the mussels in a colander.

Pour the wine into a wide pan, add the same quantity of water, the shallot, parsley stalks and bay leaf. Bring to the boil and simmer for 2 minutes. Add the mussels and cover. Shake the pan over high heat for 1 minute then remove from the heat and leave, covered, for 5 minutes to allow the mussels to open. Discard any that do not open. The cooking juices can be strained and reserved as fish stock.

Meanwhile toast the almonds in a preheated oven or under a high grill until golden then chop them fairly finely in a processor or blender. Tip two-thirds of the almonds into a bowl and grind the remainder until a fine powder. Add to the bowl with the softened butter, lemon juice and chopped coriander and blend until spreadable.

Discard one of the shells from each opened mussel and spread a little almond butter over the mussel in the other shell. Divide the mussels between 4 *gratin* dishes and set them aside in a cold place until ready to serve.

Place the dishes on a baking sheet, cook in a preheated oven for 4-6 minutes until the butter has melted and the mussels are piping hot. Serve straight away with fresh bread to soak up the juices.

∽

Right
M U S S E L S   W I T H   A L M O N D   A N D
C O R I A N D E R   B U T T E R

Marinated Mediterranean Prawns
en brochette

The Spanish idea of steeping prawns in seasoned sherry produces an excellent flavour.

S E R V E S   2 - 4

16-20 Mediterranean prawns, cooked in their shells

8-12 fresh bay leaves

2 tablespoons Manzanilla sherry

2 tablespoons extra virgin olive oil

8 cloves, roughly crushed in a mortar

salt and freshly milled black pepper

2 tablespoons finely chopped coriander or parsley

225 g / 8 oz freshly cooked long-grain rice

a little extra olive oil

4 metal *brochettes* or wooden skewers

O V E N

200°C 400°F Gas Mark 6 Roasting Oven

Peel the body of the prawns but leave the tails intact, remove any fine black lines of the intestines and briefly rinse the shellfish in cold water. Dry on kitchen paper. Arrange the prawns in a single layer in a shallow dish with the bay leaves.

Mix the sherry with the olive oil, cloves, salt, pepper and chopped coriander or parsley. Pour over the prawns and the bay leaves making sure that all surfaces are coated with the marinade. Cover and chill for 2-6 hours. Thread the prawns and the bay leaves on to 4 metal *brochettes* or wooden skewers soaked in water for half an hour to prevent burning.

Spread the hot rice in an even layer in a lightly-oiled oven dish. Arrange the *brochettes* on top and spoon any marinade over them. Place in a hot oven – or under a hot grill – for 4-5 minutes until the prawns are heated through. Serve straight away.

Crab and Fennel Tart

Devon crabs are one of Britain's finest foods. When short of time, I buy freshly-prepared crab meat from my local fishmonger since in this delectable tart the white and brown crab meat are mixed together.

S E R V E S   6

170 g / 6 oz prepared-weight shortcrust pastry

knob of butter

3 eggs

225 g / 8 oz prepared crab meat, or the meat from a 900 g / 2 lb crab

150 g / 5 fl oz double cream

30 g / 1 oz freshly grated Parmesan cheese

1-2 teaspoons finely chopped herb fennel or dill

¼ teaspoon finely grated zest of lemon

salt and freshly grated nutmeg

O V E N

200°C 400°F Gas Mark 6 Roasting Oven
190°C 375°F Gas Mark 5
Baking or Roasting Oven

Roll out the pastry to line a buttered 23cm / 9in fluted tart tin. Separate 2 of the eggs and lightly whisk the whites. Brush a little egg white over the inside of the pastry case and prick lightly all over. Bake in the preheated oven for 8-10 minutes until the pastry is set.

Meanwhile, mix the crab meat with the 2 egg yolks and the remaining whole egg. Stir in the cream, cheese, fennel or dill and zest of lemon. Season the mixture with salt and nutmeg. Whisk the remaining egg whites until stiff and fold in carefully.

Pour the mixture into the pastry case and return to the oven. Bake for 5 minutes then, if possible, turn down the heat to the lower temperature, and bake for a further 30-35 minutes until the filling is puffed up and is just set in the centre. Serve immediately.

~

DEVILLED CRAB
WITH HOT AVOCADO PEAR

Devon crabs are so plentiful that each summer I devise new ways of serving them. This partnership works specially well.

SERVES 4

900 g / 2 lb crab or 450 g / 1 lb prepared crab meat

150 ml / 5 fl oz soured cream

1 teaspoon plain Dijon mustard

1-2 teaspoons Meaux or Dijon seed mustard

⅛ teaspoon ground fenugreek

⅛ teaspoon cayenne pepper

½ teaspoon grated lemon zest

juice of 1 large lemon

2 ripe avocado pears

30 g / 1 oz butter

slim clove of garlic, peeled and crushed

1 teaspoon each of finely chopped parsley, and coriander or dill

GARNISH

4 wedges of lemon

OVEN

200°C 400°F Gas Mark 6 Roasting Oven

Prepare the crab in the usual way by discarding the inedible parts and extracting the white and brown crab meat, keeping the meats separate.

Mix the soured cream with both mustards, the fenugreek and the cayenne pepper. Add the zest of lemon and sufficient juice to slightly sharpen yet balance the flavours. Combine with the white crab meat. Stir a little lemon juice into the brown crab meat.

Quarter the avocado pears then remove the stone and the peel. Form each quarter into a fan by making 4-5 lengthwise cuts leaving the pear joined at the stalk or narrow end and flattening slightly with the palm of your hand to spread the slices out.

Butter 4 small *gratin* dishes and arrange 2 fans of avocado on each. Melt the butter in a pan and stir in the garlic and herbs, then spoon over the avocado pears. Cover each dish with a butter paper or a piece of foil.

Place the dishes in a preheated oven for 7 minutes until heated through. Take care not to overcook the avocado or the flavour will be bitter. Remove from the oven, make a space between the fans and spoon a quarter of each crab meat on to each dish. Garnish with lemon wedges and serve straight away with warm bread or rolls.

~

Roast Lobster
with Thai Herb Butter

*This is one of the most delicious ways of
cooking a lobster for eating hot. If
you can't bring yourself to deal with the live
lobster at home, ask your fishmonger to
do it, then place the cleaned, oven-ready
halves in a container, surrounded
by ice, and hurry home to cook it straight
away. As it cooks, the blue-black shell
of the lobster turns the familiar coral pink.*

S E R V E S   2

T H A I   H E R B   B U T T E R
100 g / 3½ oz finest unsalted butter

2 stems lemon grass, trimmed and peeled of
outer leaves

hazelnut-size piece of peeled fresh ginger, grated

1 tablespoon coriander leaves, chopped

1 tablespoon basil leaves

¼ teaspoon chopped fresh red or green chilli
pepper (optional)

zest and juice of ½ lime

1 kg / 2 lb live lobster

salt

O v e n
200°C 400°F Gas Mark 6 Roasting Oven

Melt the butter in a small pan and add the
lemon grass (cut into short lengths and gently bruised in a mortar), with the ginger and
leave in a warm place for 30 minutes to
allow the flavours to infuse the butter. Strain
the butter into another pan and then add the
coriander, basil, chilli pepper and zest and
juice of lime. Keep warm, the butter should
remain soft.

Now to tackle the lobster. I feel safer
wearing old leather gloves but they are not
essential. Place the lobster on a folded cloth
on a wooden board, and look for the cross-
shaped mark on the top of the shell, just
behind the head. To kill the lobster, plunge
the pointed blade of a heavy sharp knife into
the centre of the cross. Now cut down
through the shell to halve the head and then
the body, into two neat pieces. Turn over the
halves and remove the grey-green 'sack' at
the top of the head, and also the black
thread of intestines down through the tail.
When roasting the body, it is better to detach
the claws and boil them in salted water for
20 minutes.

Place the two halves of lobster on one or
two oven dishes – if necessary, support them
with crumpled foil to keep the lobster level.
Spoon some of the prepared butter over each
half of lobster. Roast in the preheated oven
for 15-20 minutes basting the lobster meat
with more butter half way through. Serve
straight away, with the cracked claws, and
any remaining butter poured into a dish.

≈

Right
R O A S T   L O B S T E R   W I T H   T H A I
H E R B   B U T T E R

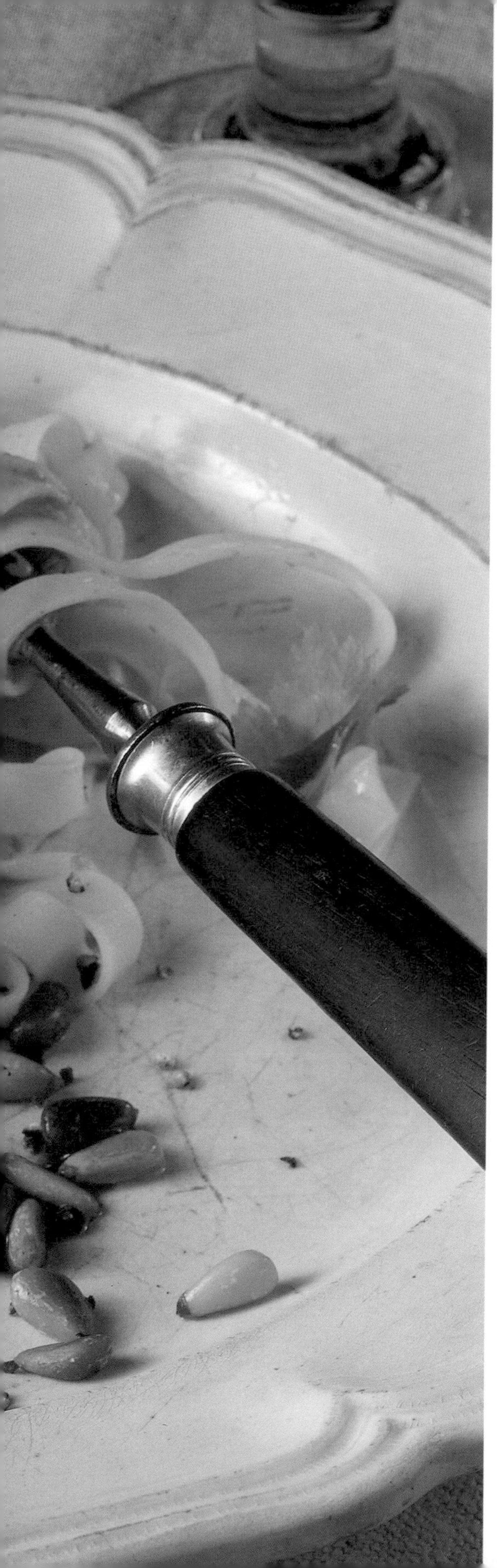

CHAPTER 3

PASTA AND RICE

Savoury dishes of pasta and rice are now part of British home cooking. We have taken to our hearts these staple foods from Italy and the Orient, often combining them in new ways with vegetables, nuts or sauces that can be piquant or creamy, or rich with our native herbs.

Left

PASTA WITH ROASTED RED PEPPER, GARLIC AND PINE NUT SAUCE

page 55

In her chapter on Oven Cookery, the incomparable Eliza Acton writes, 'Rice is most excellent when thus slowly baked with a certain proportion of liquid, either by itself, or mingled with meat, fish, or fruit'. Indeed, oven-cooked rice has every advantage – the method is simple, the rice does not stick to the pan, and the results are perfect.

Ever since Len Deighton's brilliant newspaper cook strip appeared in the sixties, I have followed his recommendation for preparing plain boiled rice: to serve two people, pour a mug of white – ie polished – long-grain rice into a sieve and wash it well under cold, running water for 4-5 minutes or until the liquid running from the sieve is clear. Tip the washed rice into a heavy-based pan or casserole, and add cold water or stock to cover by 0.5 cm / ¼ in. In practice this usually means adding the same *volume* of cooking water as of dry rice. I usually add a bay leaf, a few cloves, a slice of onion and a knob of butter, but this is a matter of personal choice. Bring the rice and water to the boil on the hob, stir well, and cover with a tight-fitting lid. Transfer to a moderate oven (140°C 275°F Gas Mark 1 Simmering Oven), and cook for 20 minutes. Remove the rice from the oven and leave, covered, for 10 minutes before serving.

This basic recipe is capable of many variations: the rice can be spiced by adding a piece of cinnamon bark, some coriander seeds and a few bruised cardamom pods to the cooking water. Or a most delicious rice to accompany Indian, Thai and Indonesian dishes is prepared by cooking the rice in coconut milk with a little crushed garlic, some chopped lemon grass and a little grated fresh ginger.

Dried pasta, too, can be cooked in an oven. Tubular pasta like *cannelloni*, filled with a savoury mixture and covered with a well-flavoured sauce, is baked in a hot oven until cooked. Similarly, an oven-baked lasagne made with flat sheets of pasta – either used straight from the packet or first softened in boiling water for 2 minutes – and layered with a savoury filling of fish, meat or vegetables and covered with a béchamel sauce, is baked in a preheated oven until bubbling and aromatic.

Shaped pasta like ridged *fusilli*, shell-shaped *conchiglie* and ribbon pasta such as *tagliatelle* and *pappardelle*, can be cooked very easily in a preheated oven. Into a large pan of salted boiling water, add the pasta – allowing about 85 g / 3 oz per person – and bring back to the boil for 1 minute. Cover with a lid and transfer to a hot oven, then cook for the time recommended on the packet. Drain the pasta and dress with melted butter or olive oil and plenty of freshly grated Parmesan cheese and black pepper, or a well-flavoured sauce (such as one of the four classic suggestions I have given here).

Roasted Red Pepper, Garlic and Pine Nut Sauce

This rich red sauce goes well with pasta, baked potatoes and grilled chicken.

Serves 4

4 sweet red peppers

4-6 fat cloves of garlic

6-8 tablespoons olive oil

1-2 tablespoons balsamic vinegar

salt

55 g / 2 oz pine nuts, lightly toasted in the oven

Oven

200°C 400°F Gas Mark 6 Roasting Oven

Wash and dry the peppers, separate the cloves of garlic but leave in their papery skins. Place the peppers and garlic in a lightly-oiled cast-iron dish. Roast in the preheated oven for 30 minutes turning them over now and again, do not worry if the skin blackens in places. Remove from the oven and cover with an upturned bowl so that the condensation loosens the skin on the peppers and mellows the roasting juices in the pan.

Cut the peppers in half, discard any blackened areas of the skin, leaving the rest intact, discard the stalks and seeds. Peel the garlic. In a processor or blender, purée the peppers and garlic with the cooking juices from the pan and half the olive oil until fairly smooth. Mix in the remaining olive oil and sufficient balsamic vinegar to give a slightly piquant flavour, then season with salt. Spoon the sauce into a bowl and mix in the pine nuts.

Anchoiade

This piquant anchovy and garlic sauce from Provence goes well with warm crusty bread, hot boiled potatoes or a dish of freshly cooked tagliatelle. The fresh figs in the recipe are optional, they appear in the sauce in some areas of Provence but not others.

Serves 4

45 g / 1¾ oz tin anchovy fillets in olive oil

2-3 cloves garlic, peeled and crushed or chopped

1 tablespoon capers, chopped

1-2 fresh figs, roughly chopped (optional)

freshly milled black pepper

ground coriander seeds

3-4 tablespoons olive oil

red wine vinegar to taste

Use a pestle and mortar, or a blender or food processor, to crush together the anchovies, garlic and capers with the figs, if available. Add a little milled black pepper and some ground coriander, and gradually incorporate the olive oil to make a fairly smooth purée. Slightly sharpen the flavour with a dash of wine vinegar. Pour into a small china bowl, cover and chill until ready to serve. The flavour of the sauce improves if made 1-2 days ahead. The sauce can be thinned with warm water if desired.

WALNUT AND GARLIC SAUCE

*A good, simple sauce from the Toulouse
region of France. Serve over hot
pasta or to accompany a platter of* crudités,
*(small fingers of raw vegetables such
as celery, carrot, chicory, sweet peppers and
Florence fennel).*

S E R V E S   4

85 g / 3 oz shelled walnuts
boiling water
2-3 cloves of garlic, peeled
85-150 ml / 3-5 fl oz fruity olive oil
2-4 tablespoons hot water
salt
dash of sherry vinegar or lemon juice
walnut oil

Cover the walnuts with boiling water, drain
and rinse in cold water and dry on kitchen
paper. If you wish, peel the walnuts, but
unless the skin is bitter-tasting I usually leave
them unpeeled.

Chop the nuts and the garlic in a processor
with the oil and some of the water to make a
not too smooth purée. Add a little extra
water if the sauce is too thick. Spoon into a
bowl, season to taste with salt and a dash of
sherry vinegar or lemon juice. Stir in a little
walnut oil to give a rich flavour. Cover and
set aside until needed.

~

PESTO

*The original basil-rich version of this
classic Genoese sauce remains far and
away the best.*

S E R V E S   4

100 g / 3½ oz basil leaves
8 tablespoons olive oil
30 g / 1 oz pine nuts
1-2 cloves of garlic, peeled and crushed
55 g / 2 oz Parmesan cheese, finely grated

Put the basil, olive oil, pine nuts and garlic
into the bowl of a food processor, blender or
mortar and blend to a paste. Add the cheese
and mix briefly to incorporate it. Scrape the
pesto into a bowl and set aside, covered, in a
cold place until needed.

~

SAFFRON ORZO

*Orzo is the rice-shaped pasta from
Calabria – the most southern toe of Italy.
This luxurious version
prepared with cream and saffron makes a
fine accompaniment to game.*

S E R V E S   6 - 8

450 g / 1 lb orzo
boiling water
salt
2 generous pinches saffron threads
2 tablespoons hot water
30 g / 1 oz butter

1 tablespoon finely chopped onion

sliver of garlic, finely chopped

150 ml / 5 fl oz double cream

3 fresh bay leaves

finely grated zest and juice of 1 lemon

GARNISH

sprigs of fresh bay leaves

OVEN

150°C 300°F Gas Mark 2 Simmering Oven

Sprinkle the orzo into a large pan of salted boiling water. Bring back to the boil, cover and place in the preheated oven for 15 minutes or until almost tender. Drain, reserving a quarter of the cooking liquor.

Place the saffron threads on a saucer with the hot water and place in the preheated oven for 5 minutes. Saffron may be one of the most expensive spices, but its unique subtle taste makes this a memorable dish.

Melt the butter in a pan, stir in the onion and garlic over moderate heat for 4-5 minutes until soft and translucent. Add the saffron and water, the cream and bay leaves and stir for 2 minutes. Add the drained orzo and cook together for 5-10 minutes, adding some of the cooking water, if necessary, until the orzo is completely tender and has taken on the colour of the saffron. Add salt to taste and discard the bay leaves.

Spoon the orzo onto a warm serving dish, sprinkle lemon juice and some long slim shreds of lemon zest over the top. Garnish with fresh bay leaves and serve.

HONEYED NOODLES WITH POPPY SEEDS AND WALNUTS

In Austria the versatile noodle is served as a pudding.

SERVES 4

225 g / 8 oz dried pasta noodles

boiling water

salt

55 g / 2 oz walnut pieces

55 g / 2 oz demerara sugar

¼ teaspoon ground cinnamon

55 g / 2 oz unsalted butter

4 tablespoons blue poppy seeds

2 tablespoons clear honey

2-4 tablespoons thick cream

OVEN

200°C 400°F Gas Mark 6 Roasting Oven

Add the noodles to a pan of lightly salted boiling water. Bring back to the boil, cover the pan and cook in the preheated oven for the time recommended on the packet. Drain well and tip into a hot serving dish. Keep the noodles warm.

Chop the walnuts until as coarse or fine as you wish. Mix with the sugar and cinnamon and tip into a small bowl or dish.

When the noodles are cooked, melt the butter in a pan and stir in the poppy seeds for 1-2 minutes over medium heat. Stir in the honey and cream and when combined spoon over the noodles and toss. Serve with the walnut mixture for spooning over the top.

BROWN RICE
WITH INDIAN SPICED CASHEW NUTS

*The combination of brown rice and spicy nuts
is specially appetizing and flavourful.
Cashew nuts can be replaced by hazelnuts,
walnuts or pecans if you prefer.*

S E R V E S   2

1 mug (size dependent on appetite) of brown
long-grain rice

salt

white part of a leek or a shallot,
finely chopped

bouquet of parsley, bay leaf, and thyme tied
with ½ stick of celery

200 g / 7 oz cashew nuts, plain or roasted

2 tablespoons sunflower oil

1 clove garlic, peeled and finely chopped

1 shallot, peeled and finely chopped

1 teaspoon dry garam masala eg Pataks

2 tablespoons coconut cream

150 ml / 5 fl oz tomato juice

salt and cayenne pepper

2-3 teaspoons chopped coriander leaves

fresh wedges of lime to serve / garnish

O V E N
180°C 350°F Gas Mark 4
Roasting or Simmering Oven

Measure the rice into a sieve and wash under
cold, running water for 4-5 minutes until the
liquid from the sieve is clear. Turn the rice
into a flame-proof casserole and add one and
a half times the volume of rice of cold water
or vegetable stock. Add a little salt, the leek
or shallot and bouquet of herbs. Bring the
liquid to the boil, stir the rice well and cover
with a lid. Transfer to the preheated oven
and cook for 40 minutes. Remove from the
oven and leave, covered, in a warm place for
10 minutes. The rice is properly cooked
when each grain is tender and all the liquid
has been absorbed. However, rice varies a
good deal and therefore you may need to
adjust the cooking time.

Prepare the cashew nuts by heating the oil
and cooking the garlic and shallot until soft
but not coloured. Stir in the garam masala
and cook for 1-2 minutes over a moderate
heat. Add the cashew nuts and stir until coated with the oil. Stir in the coconut cream and
the tomato juice and cook, stirring gently,
until the ingredients blend to form a sauce
for the nuts. Season to taste with salt and
cayenne pepper. At the last moment stir in
the coriander leaves. Serve the cashew nuts
with the brown rice and wedges of lime and
accompany, if you like them, with a choice
of Indian pickles or chutneys.

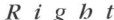

Right
B R O W N   R I C E   W I T H   I N D I A N   S P I C E D
C A S H E W   N U T S

SOUFFLED THAI RICE IN MARROW BOATS

*Thai-style rice makes a good companion
for summer courgettes.*

SERVES 4

1 teacup long-grained white rice

1 teacup cold water

bay leaf

slice of onion

salt and freshly milled black pepper

1 medium marrow or 2 overgrown courgettes

2-3 slices Italian *coppa* or streaky bacon, diced

sliver of garlic, peeled and crushed

30g / 1oz butter

1 teaspoon coriander leaves, chopped

2 eggs, separated

freshly grated nutmeg

2 tablespoons freshly grated Parmesan cheese

1 teaspoon chopped chives

OVEN

140°C 275°F Gas Mark 1 Simmering Oven

190°C 375°F Gas Mark 5 Roasting Oven

Tip the rice into a sieve and wash thoroughly under cold, running water for 4-5 minutes. In a flameproof casserole or lidded saucepan, bring the rice and water to the boil with the bay leaf, onion and some salt and pepper. Stir well, cover with a tight-fitting lid and cook in the preheated oven – at the lower temperature – for 20 minutes. When cooked, discard the bay leaf and onion.

Meanwhile, if the skin is tough, peel the marrow – courgettes are younger and may not need to be peeled. Cut in half and scoop out the seeds, cut the marrow into 4 boat-shaped pieces – the hollowed-out halves of courgette are already boat-shaped. Steam the pieces of marrow or courgette for 5-6 minutes until tender. Then arrange in one large or 4 individual buttered ovenproof dishes.

Gently fry the *coppa* or bacon and garlic in the butter for 4-5 minutes. Remove from the heat and stir in the coriander, the cooked rice and the egg yolks. Season with a little grated nutmeg. Spoon the rice into the pieces of marrow or courgette. Whisk the egg whites with a pinch of salt until stiff, fold in the cheese and chives and spoon the mixture over the rice.

Bake in the preheated oven – at the higher temperature (see above) – for 10 minutes.

SPICED RICE SALAD

*A fine Mediterranean accompaniment
to cold meat or fish.*

SERVES 6-8

450g / 1lb patna or other long-grain rice

DRESSING

½-1 clove garlic, peeled and crushed or finely chopped

½ teaspoon grated fresh ginger

¼ teaspoon ground coriander

¼ teaspoon freshly grated nutmeg

6-8 tablespoons olive oil

finely grated zest and juice of 1 lemon

salt and freshly milled green or black peppercorns

100g / 3½oz ready-to-eat apricots, cut into narrow strips

55g/2oz seedless raisins

55g/2oz currants

2 sticks green celery, diced

2-4 spring onions, chopped

55g/2oz lightly toasted pine nuts

OVEN

140°C 275°F Gas Mark 1 Simmering Oven

Cook the spiced rice by the method described on p58.

Meanwhile prepare the dressing by mixing together the garlic, ginger, coriander, nutmeg, olive oil and lemon zest and juice in the serving bowl – beat with a wooden spoon or a whisk until well combined. Season to taste with salt and milled pepper and stir in the apricots, raisins and currants.

Remove the spices from the freshly cooked rice and while it is still warm stir the rice into the dressing until evenly coated – if need be add a little more oil – and leave to cool. Then stir in the celery and spring onions and sprinkle the pine nuts over the top.

STUFFED BUTTERNUT SQUASH

Serve to accompany roast poultry and game, or on its own for vegetarians.

SERVES 4-8

1 butternut squash

a little mild salad oil

115g/4oz wild rice

300ml/10fl oz water

1 shallot, finely chopped

1 clove garlic, finely chopped

1 stick celery, finely chopped

55g/2oz butter

115g/4oz hunza apricots, cooked and stoned, or ready-to-eat apricots, roughly chopped

55g/2oz rye or wholemeal breadcrumbs

115g/4oz blanched halved almonds, toasted

55g/2oz ground almonds

finely grated zest and juice of ½ lemon

finely grated nutmeg

salt

OVEN

190°C 375°F Gas Mark 5 Roasting Oven

Wash and dry the squash, make a few holes in the skin and wrap in lightly oiled foil. Bake the squash in an ovenproof dish in the preheated oven for 50 minutes.

Bring the rice to the boil in the salted water on the hob. Cover and cook in a cast-iron casserole in the preheated oven for 50 minutes. Transfer the casserole to the hob and simmer, uncovered, for a few minutes to evaporate any surplus liquid. Tip the rice into a bowl.

In a pan, soften the shallot, garlic and celery in the butter for 5 minutes. Add to the rice with the roughly chopped apricots, breadcrumbs, toasted almonds and ground almonds. Mix in the lemon zest and juice and season to taste with nutmeg and salt.

Halve the squash lengthways, remove the seeds and place the halves in a lightly oiled ovenproof dish. Spoon the stuffing into the squash, cover each half with buttered paper and reheat in a hot oven for 15-20 minutes. To serve, scoop out the squash with some stuffing.

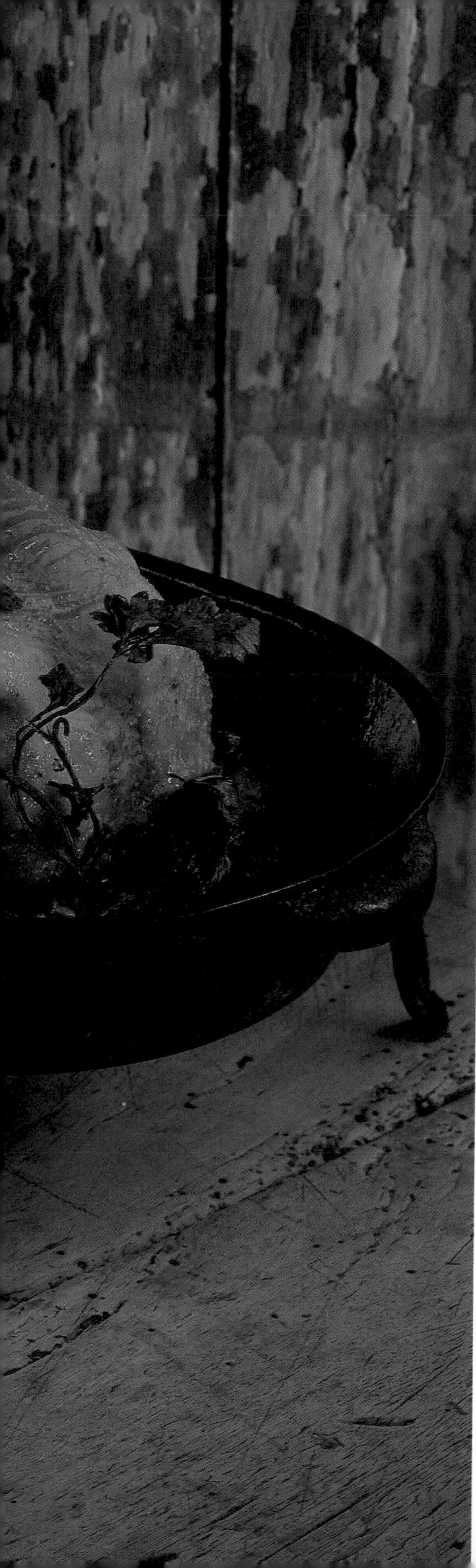

CHAPTER 4

MEAT AND POULTRY

No dish evokes our culinary heritage quite so compellingly as a magnificent joint of roasted meat. Visions of a baron of beef or a leg of lamb, turning slowly on a spit, pass before one's eye, the golden-brown gleaming crust concealing the moist, succulent meat inside.

Left
SIMPLE ROAST CHICKEN STUFFED WITH HERBS *page 79*

ROASTED meat is the epitome of traditional oven cooking. Yet – funds permitting – no dish is easier to achieve. For the most successful result, buy as large a piece of meat as you can afford, ideally one that will provide servings of both hot and cold roasted meat. Whenever possible, have the meat left on the bone, for the bones not only contribute a unique flavour but also transmit the heat into the joint.

Far more important than any fancy treatment before or after cooking, is that meat for roasting should be properly aged – or hung – before it is put into the oven. The colour of the meat is an indication of its age. Beef, in particular, should be a deep crimson rather than bright pillar-box red. If your meat is home-reared and slaughtered then you can decide how long to age the carcase before butchering. Otherwise, patronize a butcher whose meat you can trust and with whom you can discuss the provenance and quality of his produce. If, though, you have some meat that you suspect needs to be hung longer, then place it on a piece of folded kitchen paper on a plate, in the bottom of the fridge for 1-2 days. This allows the natural enzymes in the meat extra time to break down the cellular structure and so tenderize the joint. An alternative way to tenderize and flavour meat is to marinate it for 2-4 days in a mixture of wine, herbs and seasonings as in a classic *daube de boeuf.*

Although pork and poultry should always be well-cooked, how rare or well-done you like roasted beef, lamb and veal is a matter of personal preference. That said, it is essential to rest roasted meat for 20-30 minutes – ideally in a warm place – after it is taken from the oven and before you carve it. In this way, the juices which the heat has drawn to the surface during roasting seep back into the flesh, a process that is sometimes described as allowing the meat to relax.

Achieving the desired degree of roasting is much easier if you cook the meat with a meat thermometer impaled in the thickest part. Experience will tell you how to interpret the temperatures shown on the dial but it's worth remembering that meat continues to cook for a short time even after removing it from the oven.

Roasted meat that is intended to be served cold should be cooked only a few hours ahead and be stored, ideally, in a cold pantry rather than the fridge. Marvellous earthenware *tagines* or casseroles are available from the Elizabeth David Cookshop, 3 North Row, The Market, London WC2E 8RA.

MEAT ROASTING

All meat should be at room temperature before being placed in the oven. The times given below are given as a rough guide since the dimensions of a joint clearly affect its cooking time, for example, a long narrow piece of meat cooks in less time than a thick squat joint. Pat all meat dry with kitchen paper then place in a roasting tin. Cook according to the guide times given below, basting the meat with the cooking juices several times during roasting. Meat with a high proportion of fat, and especially poultry such as goose and duck, should be placed on a rack in the roasting tin. From time to time during roasting, the liquid fat should be carefully poured or spooned into a bowl, and set aside for other cooking. An alternative to roasting a joint of meat at the same temperature for the whole time, is to roast it for half the time at a high temperature and then for two-thirds of the time at a lower temperature. This method can produce a tender joint with a good flavour and less shrinkage.

OVEN
200°C 400°F Gas Mark 6 Roasting Oven

BEEF
well-cooked
allow 20 minutes per 450g / 1 lb
and 20 minutes over
medium
allow 15 minutes per 450g / 1 lb
and 15 minutes over
rare
allow 12 minutes per 450g / 1 lb
and 12 minutes over

CHICKEN
allow 20 minutes per 450g / 1 lb

DUCK
allow 15-20 minutes per 450g / 1 lb

GOOSE
allow 18-20 minutes per 450g / 1 lb

LAMB AND MUTTON
well-cooked
allow 20 minutes per 450g / 1 lb
and 20 minutes over
pink
allow 18 minutes per 450g / 1 lb
and 18 minutes over

PORK
allow 30 minutes per 450g / 1 lb
and 15-30 minutes over

VEAL
allow 25 minutes per 450g / 1 lb
and 25 minutes over

FILLET OF BEEF ROAST
WITH A CRUST OF
HORSERADISH AND MUSTARD

Topside of beef can replace the fillet in this recipe but it will take a little longer to cook.

SERVES 8-10
2 kg / 4½ lb fillet of beef
knob of butter
CRUST
6 tablespoons grain mustard
3 tablespoons grated horseradish
3 tablespoons wholewheat flour
1 teaspoon dried thyme
1 teaspoon salt
85 g / 3 oz butter, melted

OVEN
220°C 425°F Gas Mark 7 Roasting Oven

Pat the beef dry with kitchen paper and place in a buttered roasting tin. Mix together the mustard, horseradish, flour, thyme and salt. Blend in the melted butter to make a paste. Spread the mixture over the top and sides of the meat in a roughly even layer.

Roast the beef in a preheated oven for 10-15 minutes per half kilo (or per pound), depending on how pink you like roast beef. Remove from the oven and rest the meat in a warm place for a minimum of 15 minutes before carving.

DAUBE PROVENÇAL DE BOEUF

A classic – perfect for a weekend lunch.

SERVES 5-6

900 g / 2 lb topside of beef

300 ml / 10 fl oz Côtes du Rhône red wine

3 tablespoons olive oil

1-2 cloves of garlic, peeled and sliced

1 teaspoon dried *herbes de Provence*

salt and freshly ground black pepper

115 g / 4 oz smoked *lardons* or diced
streaky bacon

1 onion, chopped

225 g / 8 oz tomatoes, peeled and chopped

1 strip of orange peel

2 anchovy fillets, chopped

55 g / 2 oz black olives, pitted

OVEN
325°C 170°F Gas Mark 3 Simmering Oven

Remove any fat from the beef. In a bowl, mix the wine, olive oil, garlic, herbs and seasoning. Add the meat to the marinade and turn over. Alternatively, put the meat and the marinade in a plastic bag, seal and place in the bowl. Leave in the refrigerator for one or two days, turning over now and again.

Cook the *lardons* or bacon with the onion in a cast-iron casserole until the fat runs. Add the beef and sear lightly. Add the marinade, tomatoes, orange peel and anchovies, and bring to the boil. Cover with a tight-fitting lid and cook in a preheated oven for 2-3 hours or until the meat is tender. Add the olives 10 minutes before serving. Slice the beef, serve with the sauce, plain boiled rice or noodles.

~

FILLET STEAK
WITH ROQUEFORT CHEESE

*A richly-flavoured dish from the traditional
repertoire of French cooking. Make
the rest of the meal very plain and simple,
and do not plan to work afterwards.*

SERVES 2

2 thick slices of fillet steak

freshly milled black pepper

a knob of butter

4 tablespoons brandy

55 g / 2 oz Roquefort cheese

100-150 ml / 3½-5 fl oz *crème fraîche*

OVEN
220°C 425°F Gas Mark 7 Roasting Oven

Season the steak with pepper. Melt the butter in a heavy-based skillet and sear the meat on both sides. Cook in the preheated oven, or on the hob, according to your preference.

Move the pan to the hob, pour in the brandy and set light to it. When the flames have died down, transfer the steak to a hot serving dish. Add the Roquefort cheese to the pan and stir until melted. Stir in the *crème fraîche* and allow the sauce to bubble and thicken slightly. Taste and season accordingly.

Spoon the sauce over the steak and serve with boiled or puréed potatoes.

~

Right
FILLET STEAK WITH ROQUEFORT
CHEESE

BRAISED OXTAIL
WITH BLACK GRAPES

Known in France as Queue de Boeuf à la Vigneronne, *the slight sharpness of the grapes is a marvellous foil for the rich flavour of oxtail. In late summer, I make the dish with ripe damsons in place of grapes. The fruit contributes a deeper flavour and a handsome colour. By making the dish a day ahead the flavour improves and any surplus fat is easily removed.*

SERVES 4-6

2 oxtails, jointed

salt and freshly milled black pepper

2 onions, chopped

1 clove of garlic, peeled and chopped

2 carrots, peeled and chopped

2 sticks celery, chopped

bouquet of fresh herbs

½ stick of cinnamon

600 ml / 1 pint French red wine

340 g / 12 oz black grapes, seedless or halved and deseeded

OVEN

160°C 325°F Gas Mark 3 Simmering Oven

In a heavy-based pan or casserole season the oxtails with salt and pepper, then sear the pieces until the fat begins to run. Transfer to a hot plate and soften the onions and garlic in the remaining fat in the pan. Add the carrots and celery and stir around for 2-3 minutes to soften a little.

Arrange the oxtail on top of the vegetables if possible in a single layer, and add the bouquet of herbs, the cinnamon stick and the wine. If necessary add hot water until the meat is covered.

Cover with a tight-fitting lid and cook in the preheated oven for about 3 hours. After 2 hours check that the level of the liquid has not fallen below the meat. When the meat parts easily from the bone, remove the casserole from the oven and pour the liquor into a jug. Cool then chill both the oxtails and the cooking liquid.

Next day, reheat the oxtails in the casserole in the oven. Remove the layer of fat from the jellied liquor, turn the jelly into a pan and boil steadily over high heat until reduced to half its volume and the flavour is intensifed. Pour over the oxtail, add the black grapes and cook in the preheated oven for 10-15 minutes. Serve with buttery creamed potatoes.

~

Right
BRAISED OXTAIL
WITH BLACK GRAPES

Steak and Kidney Pie with Wild Mushrooms

Wild mushrooms – even the-easy-to-spot field mushroom – have a far more intense and delicious flavour than the cultivated variety for this richly-flavoured pie.

Serves 4-5

680 g / 1½ lb trimmed chuck steak

2 tablespoons flour seasoned with salt and freshly milled black pepper

1-2 tablespoons beef dripping or butter

1-2 medium-sized onions, peeled and chopped

300 ml / 10 fl oz beer or stout

½ teaspoon finely chopped fresh thyme

170-225 g / 6-8 oz ox kidney

about 170-225 g / 6-8 oz wild mushrooms, trimmed and wiped clean

400 g / 14 oz flaky pastry

1 egg yolk for glazing the pastry

Oven

180°C 350°F Gas Mark 4 Simmering Oven

200°C 400°F Gas Mark 6
Baking or Roasting Oven

Cut the steak into 5 cm / 2 in pieces and toss in the seasoned flour until lightly coated. Melt half the dripping or butter in a pan and lightly brown the meat all over – do this in batches if necessary. Transfer the meat to a pie dish. Add the remaining fat to the pan and soften the onions for 4-5 minutes until they are just changing colour. Spoon the onions over the beef. Deglaze the pan with the beer mixed with 300 ml / 10 fl oz water and then pour over the beef. Cover the pie dish with foil, securing the edges firmly, and place in

the preheated oven for 1½-2 hours or until the beef is cooked.

Remove the pie dish from the oven and raise the temperature of the oven. Check the flavour of the gravy that has formed. Stir in the thyme and, if necessary, a little extra beer or stout.

Trim the kidney, removing the white core and any fat, and cut into 2.5 cm / 1 in pieces. Slice any large wild mushrooms, otherwise leave them whole and add them with the kidney to the beef. If you wish, place a pie funnel in the centre of the dish – the funnel allows the steam from the filling to escape and also helps to keep the pastry raised above the filling so that it stays crisp.

Roll out the pastry about 5 cm / 2 in larger than the dish. Trim off a thin strip about 1-2.5 cm / ½-1 in wide from the edge. Dampen the rim of the pie dish, then press pastry strip on to it. If using a funnel, cut a small vent in the pastry lid so that the top protrudes through the pastry. Trim off the surplus pastry and press the edges on to the pie dish, using your fingers or the tines of a fork to decorate the edge. Brush the pastry with egg yolk mixed with 1 teaspoon of cold water and, if not using a pie funnel, cut two or three steam vents in the pastry. Bake in the preheated oven for 25-30 minutes or until the pastry is crisp and golden. Remove the pie from the oven and serve immediately.

∼

HERB-CRUSTED LOIN OF LAMB

This dish is particularly suited to entertaining: everything can be prepared ahead, and the lamb is roasted quite briefly just before the meal.

SERVES 4

570 g / 1¼ lb boned loin of lamb
salt and milled pepper
small knob of butter
115 g / 4 oz fresh white bread, crusts removed
½ teacup mixed chopped fresh herbs: parsley, chervil, chives, tarragon, mint
finely grated zest and juice of ½ lemon
55 g / 2 oz melted butter
1-2 tablespoons white wine or cold water
a little extra wine

OVEN

220°C 425°F Gas Mark 7 Roasting Oven

Using a sharp knife, cut off any surplus fat just leaving a thin layer over the meat. Lightly score the fat in a criss-cross pattern with a knife and then season with salt and pepper. Place the loin of lamb in a lightly buttered roasting pan.

Crumble the bread into the bowl of a food processor, add herbs, cover and process until the mixture forms green crumbs. Add the lemon zest and juice, some salt and pepper, and the melted butter. Process again, adding a little wine or water if necessary, until the mixture lightly binds together.

Press spoonfuls of the herb crust in an even layer over the joint leaving the underside uncovered. Roast in the preheated oven for 20-25 minutes depending on how pink you like lamb. Rest the meat for 10 minutes in a warm place before serving.

Carve the lamb into slices *(noisettes)* and serve with the roasting juices heated with a splash of white wine to make a gravy. Accompany with HERB POLENTA (see p121) or new potatoes.

KIDNEYS
ROASTED IN THEIR SHIRTS

Surely the simplest of ways to cook a kidney – they are just roasted in their natural covering of suet. The result is highly delicious.

SERVES 2

6 lamb's kidneys still in their covering of fat
Maldon salt flakes

OVEN

200°C 400°F Gas Mark 6 Roasting Oven

Place the kidneys on a rack or trivet in a roasting pan. Roast in the preheated oven for 15-20 minutes or until all the fat has melted. Pour off the melted fat, and keep it for roasting potatoes on another occasion. Transfer the kidneys to a serving dish and sprinkle with salt flakes.

Serve straight away with apple sauce and FONDANT POTATOES (see p119).

Tagine of Lamb with Olives and *Citrons Confits*

Jars of lemon slices preserved in oil, citrons confits, are sold by North African grocers, though since they are simple enough to prepare at home I have included the recipe.

SERVES 6

900 g / 2 lb boned leg or shoulder of lamb
salt and freshly ground pepper
4 tablespoons fruity olive oil
1 onion, peeled and sliced
1-2 cloves of garlic, peeled and chopped
1 bouquet of fresh coriander leaves
piece of cinnamon stick
¼ teaspoon ground ginger
12 slices of *citrons confits*
120 g / 4½ oz green olives, drained
1 teaspoon orange flower water

GARNISH

1 tablespoon coriander leaves

OVEN

170°C 325°F Gas Mark 3 Simmering Oven

Remove any surplus fat from the lamb and cut the meat into 5 cm / 2 in pieces. Season the meat lightly and place in the base of a *tagine* or a casserole. Add the oil, onion, garlic, coriander, cinnamon and ginger and enough water to almost cover the meat. Cook in the preheated oven for 2 hours or until the meat is tender. If necessary remove the lid for the last 30 minutes of cooking in order to reduce the sauce.

When the meat is cooked remove and discard the coriander and cinnamon and add the *citrons confits*, cover and cook for an extra 30 minutes, adding the olives for the final 10 minutes. The dish should be served sizzling hot, straight from the oven. Just before serving, pour the orange flower water over the meat and garnish with coriander leaves. Serve with couscous or boiled rice.

~

Preserved Lemons or *Citrons Confits*

6-8 lemons, preferably organically grown and unsprayed
55 g / 2 oz cooking salt
ground medium-hot paprika
olive or sunflower oil

Wash and dry the lemons, then cut into slices discarding the pips. Layer the slices with the salt in a colander placed on a dish and set aside in a cool place for 24 hours or until the lemons have softened. Sprinkle the lemon slices with a little paprika and pack them into preserving jars. Cover with the oil and seal the jar tightly. Store in a cold place for at least 3 weeks before using.

~

Right
TAGINE OF LAMB WITH OLIVES
AND *CITRONS CONFITS*

Butterflied Lamb
with Yoghurt and Ginger

In this Middle Eastern recipe, the boned meat is marinated in yoghurt and fresh ginger – a beautifully flavoured alternative to the more usual wine-based marinade of southern Europe.

SERVES 8

2.75 kg / 6 lb leg of lamb

MARINADE

300 ml / 10 fl oz natural yoghurt
5 cm / 2 in piece fresh ginger, peeled and grated
finely grated zest of 1 small lemon or lime
1-2 cloves of garlic, peeled and crushed
salt and freshly milled black pepper

OVEN

200°C 400°F Gas Mark 6 Roasting Oven

Either ask your butcher to bone the meat or using a small, sharp knife (a boning knife is sold specifically for this task), follow the line of the bone down through the leg of lamb cutting away the meat in short even strokes. The bone should come away cleanly. The resulting shape of the lamb is said to resemble a butterfly. Now bat out the meat, using a wooden mallet or a rolling-pin, until it is roughly 5 cm / 2 in thick all over.

Mix all the ingredients for the marinade in a bowl. Place the meat, skin-side down, on the lightly oiled grid of a roasting tin or grill pan. Spoon the marinade over the meat, making sure the whole surface is covered. Leave in a cold place for 4-8 hours.

Cook the meat in a preheated oven for about 30 minutes – when it will be still pink and succulent, or for a little longer and cooked to your preference – and the marinade is starting to brown in places. Transfer the meat to a carving board and cut across into slices for serving.

Shoulder of Lamb
stuffed with Spinach and Pine Nuts

Inspired by a recipe in Robert May's The Accomplished Cook *(1685), this dish – though it looks complicated – is quite simple and makes a fine centre-piece for a weekend lunch.*

SERVES 6-8

1.5 kg / 3½ lb boned shoulder of lamb
1 teaspoon coriander seeds, finely ground
1 teaspoon ground mace
½ teaspoon grated nutmeg
½ teaspoon salt
hazelnut-sized piece of fresh ginger, grated
knob of butter
½ teaspoon coarse salt

STUFFING

225 g / 8 oz young spinach leaves
115 g / 4 oz mixed fresh herbs: parsley, sorrel, chervil, tarragon, fennel, lemon thyme and watercress
55 g / 2 oz fresh breadcrumbs, white or wholemeal
55 g / 2 oz stoned, ready-to-eat prunes, chopped
30 g / 1 oz currants
1 teaspoon salt

1 clove garlic, peeled and chopped

1 small shallot, peeled and chopped

55 g / 2 oz butter

55 g / 2 oz pine nuts

grated zest and juice of ½ lemon

1 egg, beaten

O V E N

200°C 400°F Gas Mark 6 Roasting Oven

180°C 350°F Gas Mark 4
Baking or Simmering Oven

Place the meat skin-side down on a chopping board. Mix the spices with the salt and fresh ginger, sprinkle over the surface of the meat and rub in to season it well. Remove the stalks from the spinach and herbs, and roughly chop them. Mix in a bowl with the breadcrumbs, prunes, currants and salt. Soften the garlic and shallot in the butter, stir in the pine nuts for 2 minutes but do not allow them to burn, then add to the bowl with the lemon zest and juice, mixed with the egg. Stir until all the ingredients are combined. Spoon on to the meat, pressing it in to the folds.

Starting with the more ragged end, roll up the meat, neatly enclosing the stuffing. Secure with needle skewers, and tie securely with string in 5 or 6 places. Place the joint in a roasting pan and rub the knob of butter over the surface, sprinkle with sea salt.

Roast in a preheated oven for 1 hour. Then cook at the lower temperature for 30-45 minutes, or until cooked right through. Transfer the meat to a carving-plate or board. Rest in a warm place for 15 minutes before carving. When serving hot, cut into 6-8 thick pieces; when serving cold, carve into thinner slices.

ROAST LEG OF LAMB
WITH ROSEMARY AND GARLIC

A simple but excellent method of roasting a leg of lamb. The flavours of the herb penetrate the meat so that the lamb tastes equally delicious served hot or cold.

S E R V E S   8 - 1 0

1 leg of lamb

6 cloves of garlic, peeled

6 anchovy fillets (optional)

6 sprigs of fresh rosemary

2 tablespoons olive oil

salt and freshly milled pepper

150 ml / 5 fl oz dry white or rosé wine

150 ml / 5 fl oz vegetable stock or water

O V E N

180°C 350°F Gas Mark 4 Roasting Oven

Place the lamb in a roasting pan. Cut the garlic and anchovies into slivers and strip the leaves from the rosemary. Make about 20 small slits in the meat and slip in a sliver of garlic, a piece of anchovy and 2-8 rosemary leaves. Brush the meat with olive oil and season.

Roast the lamb in the preheated oven, 20 minutes per 500 g / 1 lb if you like it pink, otherwise cook it until it is to your taste.

Transfer the meat to a serving plate and rest in a warm place for 20 minutes. Meanwhile pour off the surplus fat from the roasting pan and make gravy by adding the wine and stock to the pan and simmering, stirring to incorporate the cooking juices, for 5 minutes or so until well-flavoured.

Pork Chops
with Herb Garden Salsa

*Meat cooked quite simply and then partnered
with a stunningly good sauce or fresh
salsa is an unfailingly good combination.
Derived from Mexican and Spanish
cooking, fresh salsas appeal to almost
everyone, with their aromatic flavour
and attractive colour. Make this salsa as you
need it, or at least no more than an
hour or so ahead. A robustly flavoured,
Sicilian-inspired variation is to add a
little Dijon mustard, a couple of chopped
cured anchovies and some drained capers.*

Serves 2

2 pork chops
½ teaspoon coriander seeds, finely crushed
salt and freshly milled black pepper
small knob of butter
2 tablespoons dry white wine

Salsa

1 clove garlic, peeled
½-1 small green chilli, deseeded
1½ tablespoons flat-leaf parsley
1½ tablespoons coriander seeds
2-3 tablespoons olive or sunflower oil
¼ teaspoon finely grated zest of lime
juice of ½ lime, or according to size
salt

Oven

180°C 350°F Gas Mark 4
Roasting or Baking Oven

Season the chops with coriander, salt and
pepper. Melt the butter in a heavy-based skillet, and lightly sear the meat on both sides.

Add the wine, cover with buttered paper and
cook in the preheated oven for 20-30 minutes depending on their thickness. Rest the
meat in a warm place for 5 minutes before
serving. Reserve the cooking juices.

Meanwhile finely chop the garlic with the
green chilli. Remove the leaves from the
herbs, and chop the stalks finely, then chop
the leaves a little more coarsely. Mix the
chopped ingredients with the oil and the
lime zest and juice. Season to taste with salt.

Arrange the pork chops on a serving dish
and spoon over the cooking juices (if necessary, reduce over a high heat). Spoon the
herb garden salsa beside the meat and serve
straight away.

∽

Right
Pork Chops with herb garden
salsa

PORK FILLET
STUFFED WITH APPLES, PRUNES AND WALNUTS

Pork fillet or tenderloin, in this case, flavoured with aromatic resinous juniper berries and autumn fruit and nuts, makes an excellent dish for serving cold, when it is easy to cut into attractive slices. The flavour of the dish is enhanced if you can prepare it a day ahead.

SERVES 10-12

225 g / 8 oz large juicy pitted prunes such as *pruneaux d'Agen*

300 ml / 10 fl oz freshly brewed lime or Lapsang Souchong tea, strained

2 pork fillets or tenderloins

salt and freshly milled black pepper

450 g / 1 lb best quality pork sausagemeat

1 slim clove garlic, peeled and crushed

4 juniper berries, crushed in a mortar

1 tablespoon chopped chives

2 tablespoons chopped parsley

2 tablespoons Calvados or dry white wine

1 large dessert apple, cored and diced

55 g / 2 oz walnut halves

1 teaspoon dried *herbes de Provence* or dried thyme

OVEN
190°C 375°F Gas Mark 5 Roasting Oven

Cut the prunes in half and soak them in the hot tea for 3-4 hours or until the fruit has absorbed most of the liquid.

Trim any surplus fat from the pork and hammer out each piece to a thickness of 1 cm / ½ in. Trim the ends of the meat neatly, and season all over with salt and pepper. Make the stuffing by mixing the sausagemeat with the garlic, juniper berries, chives, parsley, Calvados and apple. Season lightly.

Arrange one-third of the prunes on each pork fillet and place walnuts between them. Divide the stuffing between the fillets, spreading it in an even layer. Place the remaining prunes on top and cover with the other fillet, meat side uppermost. Tie the layers of meat with string in 5 or 6 places and sprinkle the top of the meat with *herbes de Provence* or dried thyme. Wrap the meat in lightly oiled kitchen foil and chill for up to 24 hours until ready to cook.

Roast the meat in the preheated oven for 45-55 minutes until cooked right through. Cool the meat – still in foil – and when completely cold, cut into slices.

BAKED AND GLAZED HAM

A baked ham, cooked a few days ahead, is the perfect cold meat during the Christmas season of festive eating. Simpler and more flavourful than the traditional coating of breadcrumbs is a mustard and honey glaze which bakes to an appetizing golden brown.

1 gammon or other cut of cured pork

1 onion studded with cloves

bouquet of parsley, thyme, bay leaf and piece of celery, tied together

1-2 tablespoons cloves

2 heaped tablespoons dark muscovado sugar
1 teaspoon mustard – English or French
4 tablespoons milk

O V E N
160°C 325°F Gas Mark 3 Simmering Oven

Follow your butcher's instructions on whether to soak the gammon in cold water prior to cooking. In a large casserole or a preserving pan, place the meat with the onion and bouquet of herbs. Add cold water to almost cover.

Slowly bring to the boil, then cover with a lid or foil and transfer to the preheated oven. Cook for 20-25 minutes to the 450 g / 1lb.

Remove the ham from the oven and leave until cool enough to handle. Depending on the flavour, discard the cooking liquor or reserve it for making soup. Transfer the meat to a roasting pan, and while still hot, cut off the rind leaving an even layer of fat – the thickness is a matter of personal preference. Cut a lattice design into the fat and stud each diamond shape with a clove. Blend together the sugar, mustard and milk and spoon some over the meat. Roast for 30 minutes in the preheated oven, basting with the glaze now and again until golden brown. Serve hot or cold, thinly carved. Accompany with Cumberland sauce or a spiced fruit jelly.

∾

SIMPLE ROAST CHICKEN
STUFFED WITH HERBS

*For this good, simple dish, the
best free-range chicken you can find will
guarantee its success.*

S E R V E S   4 - 6

1.5-2 kg / 3½-4½ lb roasting chicken, without giblets
a bunch of fresh mixed herbs: parsley, chives, tarragon, thyme, marjoram
55 g / 2 oz butter, softened
55-85 ml / 2-3 fl oz fruity dry white wine
55-85 ml / 2-3 fl oz fresh vegetable stock or water
salt and freshly milled pepper
1 teaspoon finely chopped fresh herbs

O V E N
190°C 375°F Gas Mark 5 Roasting Oven

Place the chicken in a roasting tin. Stuff the bunch of herbs into the cavity of the chicken and spread the butter over the breast. Roast in the preheated oven for 1-1½ hours, basting with the cooking juices from time to time. The chicken is cooked when the meat, pierced at the leg joint, produces clear juices.

Transfer the chicken to a hot serving dish, cover with a dry cloth and keep warm for 15 minutes. Meanwhile make the gravy: pour off the surplus fat from the roasting tin and add the wine and stock. Boil fast on the hob for 3-4 minutes, scraping the pan with a wooden spoon to incorporate the cooking juices and sediment. Remove from the heat, season and before serving add the chopped herbs.

∾

Spatchcocked Poussins
with Melon Salsa

*Traditionally, some game birds and poultry
were flattened and threaded on to
a revolving spit – hence spatched – to roast
before an open fire. The method
has several attractions: the cooking time is
reduced, the bird is well-cooked
right through, and the meat can be seasoned
and flavoured with various marinades,
butters and sauces either prior to or during
the cooking.*

Serves 2

2 poussins
salt and freshly milled pepper

GARLIC BUTTER

55 g / 2 oz slightly salted butter

1 slim clove garlic, peeled and crushed

1 teaspoon finely chopped parsley

squeeze of lemon juice

FOIE GRAS BUTTER

30 g / 1 oz slightly salted butter

30 g / 1 oz *foie gras* or *pâté de foie gras*

few drops of *marc* or brandy

MELON SALSA

½ small flavourful peach or green-fleshed melon,
deseeded and peeled, finely diced

1 medium-size ripe tomato, skinned, deseeded
and chopped

1 red chilli pepper, deseeded and finely
chopped

1 clove garlic, peeled and finely chopped

½ small shallot, peeled and finely chopped

2 tablespoons coriander leaves, chopped

1 teaspoon basil leaves, finely shredded

finely grated zest and juice of 1 lime

3 tablespoons olive or sunflower oil
salt to taste

OVEN
200°C 400°F Gas Mark 6 Roasting Oven

Use poultry shears or a heavy sharp knife to cut up through the backbone of each poussin, then open out flat. If necessary press down gently with the heel of your hand. Season the birds all over with salt and pepper and place skin-side up in a shallow roasting tin.

Make one of the seasoned butters by beating together all the ingredients in a mixing bowl until well blended. Spread half the butter over the skin of each poussin and roast in the preheated oven for 15 minutes. Spread over the remaining butter and cook for a further 10-15 minutes or until cooked right through, that is when only clear juices run from the leg joint.

Meanwhile prepare the melon salsa by mixing together all the ingredients in a bowl. Taste and, if necessary, adjust the seasoning or the balance of sweetness and sharpness by adding a little more lime juice or oil.

Serve the poussins straight from the oven, spoon over any cooking juices from the pan and accompany with the melon salsa and a crisp green salad.

≈

Right
SPATCHCOCKED POUSSINS WITH
MELON SALSA

Gascon-Style Chicken

*The very best kind of oven cooking
that produces a dish that is mellow flavoured
and utterly delicious.*

Serves 4-5

1.5-2 kg / 3½-4½ lb oven-ready corn-fed chicken

bouquet of fresh herbs – parsley, thyme,
tarragon, bay leaf

55 g / 2 oz butter

salt and freshly milled black pepper

40 cloves of garlic, peeled

200 ml / 7 fl oz French dry white wine

100 ml / 3½ fl oz stock or water

225 g / 8 oz plain flour

Oven
170°C 325°F Gas Mark 3 Simmering Oven

Remove the flap of fat from inside the chicken and tuck the herbs into the cavity. Spread two-thirds of the butter over the breast and legs, and season with salt and pepper. Use the remaining butter to grease a casserole, place the bird inside and scatter the cloves of garlic around it. Pour in the wine and stock or water and cover the casserole with a tight-fitting lid. Mix the flour with 2-3 tablespoons cold water to make a thick, malleable dough. Roll it into a long sausage and press it over the edge of the lid to seal the casserole.

Cook the chicken in the preheated oven for 2 hours. Remove from the oven and set the casserole aside for 10 minutes, then carry to the table and break the sealing paste to remove the lid – in this way none of the aroma is lost before you serve the dish. Carve the chicken into large pieces and serve with the garlic and cooking juices. Accompany with boiled or creamed potatoes so that the garlic and juices can be mashed into them.

Breast of Turkey
stuffed with mousseline

*For a picnic or a summer lunch this is an
alternative to sliced cold turkey.*

Serves 8

900 g-1.4 kg / 2-3 lb skinless breast of turkey

4-6 leaves of butterhead lettuce, washed and
patted dry

4 slices of prosciutto or Parma ham

Mousseline

115 g / 4 oz skinned breast of turkey, diced

225 g / 8 oz fromage frais

1 egg, size 3

¼ teaspoon salt

freshly milled black pepper

1 slice of prosciutto or Parma ham

½ teaspoon chopped fresh tarragon leaves

Oven
200°C 400°F Gas Mark 6 Roasting Oven

Use a small sharp boning knife to remove the breast bone from the meat, making sure the meat is left in one piece. Spread out the meat, skinned-side down, and cover with the lettuce leaves, pressing them down gently.

For the mousseline, finely chop the diced breast of turkey in a processor. Add the fromage frais, the egg, salt and pepper and process briefly until mixed. The mixture should be spoonable but not runny. Dice the slice of prosciutto and stir into the mixture along with the tarragon. Spoon the mixture on to the lettuce leaves and fold the turkey to enclose it, securing with fine needle skewers. Wrap the turkey roll in the slices of prosciutto and place on a lightly oiled double layer of baking foil. Fold up the foil to enclose the meat and place it in a roasting tin.

Cook the meat in the preheated oven for 50-60 minutes until the meat is cooked and the mousseline set. Remove from the oven and leave the meat to cool completely in the roasting tin. Unwrap and place the meat on a flat carving board or plate for serving. Spoon over the cooking juices and chill the meat for several hours before carving into slices.

~

Barbary Duck
WITH SICHUAN PEPPERED PEARS

The oriental spices are available from Chinese grocers and some supermarkets.

SERVES 4

1.5 kg / 3½ lb oven-ready Barbary duck
handful of fresh bay leaves
salt
30 g / 1 oz butter
1 small shallot, peeled and finely chopped
sliver of garlic, finely chopped
4 firm ripe pears such as Conference, peeled and quartered
2 teaspoons Sichuan pepper berries, finely crushed in a mortar

4 pieces of star anise
1 tablespoon clear honey
1 tablespoon white port or dry sherry

OVEN
200°C 400°F Gas Mark 6 Roasting Oven

Dry the duck and place on a rack in a roasting tin. Place the bay leaves in the cavity of the duck and sprinkle some salt over the skin. Roast the duck in the preheated oven for 1 hour then rest in a warm place such as the Simmering Oven for 10 minutes before carving. Once or twice during the roasting pour off the duck fat. Use some for roasting parboiled potatoes and parsnips to accompany the duck, the rest for cooking at other times.

About 20 minutes before serving the duck, melt the butter in a skillet or shallow pan attractive enough to be taken to the table. Gently cook the shallot and garlic for 4-5 minutes until softened but not coloured.

Meanwhile remove the cores from the pears and make 3-4 lengthways cuts in the thickest part of each piece of pear so that it resembles a fan. Add the pears to the skillet, placing them like the spokes of a wheel with the narrow ends in the centre. Spoon the crushed Sichuan pepper berries into a sieve and sprinkle half over the pears. Place the star anise in the centre and add the honey and port to the pan. Season lightly with salt. Cook gently on the hob until the pears are tender and the liquid has reduced to a syrup. Press the star anise with the back of a spoon to release its flavour into the sauce. Sprinkle over the remaining Sichuan pepper and keep the pears warm until ready to serve.

Christmas Roast Goose
with Apple and Sorrel Sauce

*To counteract the delicious richness
of roast goose, a fruity aromatic sauce is the
traditional accompaniment. I prefer
to roast goose without a stuffing. If you do
stuff the bird, it will require an extra
30-45 minutes in the oven.*

Serves 6
or more, depending upon appetite and
accompanying dishes

4 kg / 9 lb oven-ready goose, including giblets

salt

1 carrot, peeled and chopped

1 onion, peeled and finely chopped

½ stick celery, chopped

1 bay leaf

4 tablespoons of port

APPLE AND SORREL SAUCE

1 small shallot, finely chopped

30 g / 1 oz butter

680 g / 1½ lb Bramley apples, peeled and
chopped

finely grated zest and juice of a mandarin
orange

115 g / 4 oz fresh, dry sorrel leaves, chopped

45 g / 1½ oz sugar

Oven
200°C 400°F Gas Mark 6 Roasting Oven
160°C 325°F Gas Mark 3 Simmering Oven

Place the goose on a rack in a roasting tin and sprinkle salt all over the skin. Roast the goose in the preheated oven for 1½ hours. Then roast at the lower temperature for 1 hour or until the juices from the leg are clear.

During the cooking pour off the goose fat once or twice and store in a cold place for use in other dishes.

Meanwhile cook the giblets (reserve the liver for serving – chopped and sautéed in butter – with a salad of bitter leaves) with the carrot, onion, celery and bay leaf in water to cover. Cook in the oven or on the hob for 30 minutes. Then strain the liquid, reduce over high heat until 300 ml / 10 fl oz, then season to taste and reserve for making the gravy.

To make the sauce, soften the shallot in the butter in a pan. Stir in the apple with the orange juice. Cook, stirring, for 8-12 minutes until the apple is cooked and mushy. Stir in the sorrel leaves, ½ teaspoon grated zest of orange and the sugar. Cook until the sorrel has collapsed and is olive green. Remove from the heat and press through a sieve to make a smooth, green-flecked purée. Add salt, spoon into a dish and set aside.

Transfer the goose to a hot serving plate, and keep warm, covered with a cloth, for 20-30 minutes before carving. Pour off the surplus fat from the roasting tin. Add the giblet stock and the port and cook, stirring to incorporate the cooking juices, for 4-5 minutes. Taste and season accordingly. Pour into a hot gravy boat and serve with the carved roast goose.

～

Stuffed Escalopes of Chicken, Veal or Pork

A summer dish redolent of mint and lemon that is equally good served hot or cold. When sliced thinly, it makes an attractive buffet dish.

Serves 3-4

STUFFING
30g / 1 oz butter

1 shallot, finely chopped

30g / 1 oz pine nuts

55g / 2oz fine white breadcrumbs

1 teaspoon each of chopped mint, parsley and chives

finely shredded zest of ½ lemon

salt, milled pepper

ESCALOPES
4 escalopes of veal, chicken or pork

4 slices of Parma ham or very thin back bacon

knob of butter

2-3 tablespoons white wine

juice and finely shredded zest of ½ lemon

a little extra chopped mint

30g / 1 oz butter or 2 tablespoons thick cream

OVEN
190°C 375°F Gas 5 Roasting Oven

160°C 325°F Gas 3 Simmering Oven

To make the stuffing, melt the butter in a small pan and cook the shallot over moderate heat for 3-4 minutes until soft. Add the pine nuts, raise the heat and stir until the nuts are starting to change colour. Remove from the heat and cool slightly. Stir in the breadcrumbs, herbs, lemon zest and a little salt and pepper. Mix until the stuffing binds.

The escalopes for this dish should be very thin and measuring about 20×10cm / 8×4in. If neccesary bat out the meat with a wooden mallet to thin each piece. Lightly season the meat all over and place a slice of Parma ham or bacon on each escalope. Place a quarter of the stuffing on each, fairly close to one end. Carefully roll up the escalopes to enclose the stuffing. Place flap side down in a well buttered ovenproof dish. Add the white wine or juice of lemon and cover the escalopes with buttered paper.

Cook in the preheated oven for 20 minutes then at the lower temperature for 15-20 minutes. To make the sauce, pour the cooking juices into a small pan. Bring to the boil and, if necessary, simmer until you have about 4 tablespoons of liquid. Add the lemon zest and mint, and check the flavour before adding a splash of lemon juice or, possibly a jot more white wine. Pull the pan off the heat and stir in the butter, in small pieces, or the cream. Slide the escalopes on to a serving dish. When hot, cut each escalope into 5-6 pieces, when cold, you can slice them more thinly. Spoon the sauce around the sliced meat and serve.

~

CHAPTER 5

GAME

*Given man's interfering ways it's a
wonder that wild game still exists
at all. That we can still enjoy many of
the same species of birds and
beasts that our forefathers did is cause
for celebration.*

L e f t
QUAIL COOKED IN VINE LEAVES
WITH PESTO *page 101*

ALTHOUGH the numbers of capercaillie and snipe still diminish, sensible management has protected the future of the grouse and the partridge, and herds of deer once again roam over our moorlands.

Wild meat has long been respected for its unique taste and its seasonal scarcity. At times, this has made procuring it the preserve of the nobility and the rich. Today, though, most game – both furred and feathered, and either wild or farmed – is available to everyone in shops and restaurants.

Wild game has to search for its food so only the fleet-footed and wary survive for long. This results in lean, close-textured meat with a pronounced flavour. Mature wild game needs to be properly hung and slowly cooked to make it palatable. Young wild game, on the other hand, can be cooked in a wide variety of ways. There are few foods as delicious as a brace of autumn pheasant or a young wild rabbit that have feasted on the gleanings of the cornfields, adding a layer of yellow fat to the flesh making it particularly succulent and flavoursome.

Although farmed game lacks the romantic association of the wild, it benefits from a high-welfare and sustainable system of farming which produces tender and milder-flavoured meat that suits the palate of many people. Moreover, because farmed game usually costs less than wild game it is becoming a highly desirable animal protein for country and town dwellers alike.

Our national repertoire of game cookery encompasses such magnificent dishes as roast haunch of venison, jugged hare and a fine old English pigeon pie with its layer of suet puff pastry soaked in gravy and overlaid with crisp shortcrust. In the country we try to maintain this long and accomplished tradition, yet every year some of our best recipes slip into disuse. Partridge cooked in milk appeared on the bill of fare at St James's Palace for 21 January 1740. Yet this simple and effective method of cooking the fine-fleshed bird is rarely seen here – though it is still prepared in rural France.

There are two traditional ways of making wild game more tender and palatable: the first calls for an airy cold store or larder where game is suspended for 2-14 days to allow the natural enzymes in the meat to break down the cellular structure and thereby tenderize it; the second method is used once the game is cleaned and oven-ready when it is steeped in a marinade of wine and spices for 2-7 days before cooking. Both methods develop the flavour of the meat. I use marinades often, not only to tenderize wild game but to develop the flavour of farmed game and give it more character.

MARINADE FOR GAME

Game and pieces of meat can be immersed in this marinade for up to 2 days when stored in a cold place or the refrigerator. For a longer marinating period it is best to bring the marinade to the boil first, then cool before using. Since the point of marinating is to keep the liquid in contact with the meat at all times, for larger pieces of meat I find it more convenient to place both marinade and meat in a strong plastic bag then seal and store in a bowl in a cold place until ready to cook. For pale and white-fleshed game replace the red wine in the following recipe with rosé or white wine.

1 bottle of full-bodied red wine

4-6 tablespoons olive oil

1-2 cloves garlic, peeled and chopped

1 shallot, peeled and chopped

1 stick of celery, chopped

1 carrot, chopped

2-3 bay leaves

few stalks of parsley

few sprigs of thyme

sprig of rosemary

½ teaspoon black peppercorns, bruised

a little salt

strip of orange peel

2-3 tablespoons port or brandy (optional)

¼ teaspoon juniper berries, bruised (optional)

piece of cinnamon bark (optional)

Mix together all the ingredients and pour over the meat. Cover and store in a cold place turning the meat every day. When ready to cook, lift the meat from the marinade and pat dry with kitchen paper. Sear the meat all over in hot butter or oil, add the marinade and bring to the boil. Cover and cook slowly and gently in a preheated oven until the meat is tender. Transfer the meat to a hot serving dish and strain the liquid into a pan, then reduce in volume over high heat. Thicken slightly with a little butter blended with flour, check the seasoning and serve with the meat.

ROAST HARE
WITH *CREME FRAICHE*

This is a recipe from the Ardèche region of France.

S E R V E S   3 - 4

saddle of hare

½ teaspoon juniper berries, crushed

½ teaspoon crushed peppercorns

4-5 slices of smoked streaky bacon

olive oil

200 ml / 7 fl oz Ardèche syrah or full-bodied red wine

150 ml / 5 fl oz *crème fraîche*

O V E N
190°C 375°F Gas Mark 5 Roasting Oven

Wipe the meat with a damp cloth and if necessary, remove the thin bluish skin covering the meat. Press the juniper berries and peppercorns into the meat and place the bacon on top, tucking the ends underneath.

Place in a lightly oiled roasting tin and cover the meat with buttered paper or foil. Roast the meat in the preheated oven for 30-40 minutes. Remove the buttered paper, pour the wine over the meat, roast for 5-10 minutes.

Transfer the hare to a hot serving dish, cut the crisp bacon into small pieces and set aside. Simmer the liquid in the roasting tin for a few minutes, adding a splash of hot water if needed. Stir the *crème fraîche* into the pan and bring almost to the boil. Spoon the sauce over the hare and garnish with the bacon.

RABBIT PIE
WITH PARSLEY CREAM

*In the days of harvesting with horse-drawn
machinery and a throng of helpers,
the midday meal was carried out to the
working fields, so a pie filled
with tender rabbit was both seasonal
and appropriate.*

S E R V E S   4 - 6

1 medium-sized rabbit, jointed

salt and freshly milled pepper

55 g / 2 oz butter

2 spring onions, chopped

5 tablespoons fruity dry white wine

2 sprigs of thyme

2 teaspoons cornflour

300 ml / 10 fl oz *crème fraîche* or double cream

3 tablespoons finely chopped parsley

225 g / 8 oz prepared-weight puff or
shortcrust pastry

egg yolk, to glaze

O V E N

190°C 375°F Gas Mark 5 Roasting Oven

200°C 400°F Gas Mark 6 Roasting Oven

Wash the rabbit and pat dry with kitchen paper. Season the joints of meat with salt and black pepper.

Melt the butter in a frying-pan and lightly brown the rabbit joints all over. Stir in the spring onions, cook for 1 minute then add the wine and the same quantity of cold water and bring to the boil. Transfer the contents of the pan to a pie dish and add the sprigs of thyme. Cover the pie dish with a sheet of foil, sealing the edges well.

Cook the rabbit in the preheated oven for 30 minutes.

Remove the dish from the oven. In a bowl blend the cornflour with 1 tablespoon cold water then stir in the *crème fraîche* or cream, the parsley, and the cooking juices from the pie dish. Discard the sprigs of thyme and pour the parsley cream over the rabbit. If desired place a pie funnel in the centre of the dish.

On a floured board roll out the pastry about 5 cm/2 in larger than the dish. Trim off a strip about 1-2.5 cm/½-1 in wide from the edge. Dampen the rim of the pie dish, then press pastry strip on to it. Trim the edges. Make a steam vent in the centre and use any pastry trimmings to make leaves and berries to decorate the pastry lid. Brush the pastry with the egg yolk.

Bake the pie at the higher temperature in the preheated oven for 25-30 minutes until the pastry is golden brown and crisp. Serve the pie hot.

Right

R A B B I T   P I E   W I T H   P A R S L E Y   C R E A M

STUFFED RABBIT
WITH TAPENADE

*The aromatic Provençal mixture of black
olives, anchovies and capers
makes a good foil for the delicate gamey
flavour of rabbit.*

SERVES 4-6

4-6 rabbit joints, boned

salt and milled pepper

STUFFING

115 g / 4 oz white breadcrumbs

115 g / 4 oz smoked streaky bacon, finely
chopped

55 g / 2 oz black olives, roughly chopped

½ teaspoon chopped thyme

1 teaspoon chopped parsley

zest and juice of ½ lemon

1 egg, beaten

MARINADE

2 tablespoons tapenade

juice of ½ lemon

1 tablespoon olive oil

TAPENADE

115 g / 4 oz black olives

50 g / 1¾ oz anchovy fillets

4 tablespoons capers

55 g / 2 oz tuna fish

the juice of a lemon

about 100 ml / 3½ fl oz olive or sunflower oil

OVEN
200°C 400°F Gas Mark 6 Roasting Oven
150°C 300°F Gas Mark 2 Simmering Oven

Make the tapenade – cut the flesh from the
olives and discard the stones, then put in a
processor with the drained anchovy fillets,
capers and tuna fish. Blend the mixture with
half of the lemon juice. Mix to a smooth
purée, gradually adding the oil through the
lid of the processor. Check the taste and add
extra lemon juice if required to balance the
flavours. Spoon the tapenade into a small
bowl. Tapenade not needed in the recipe can
be spread on toasted slices of French bread
and served with drinks.

On a wooden board bat out each boned
joint of rabbit until the meat is a little thinner
and larger and will enclose the stuffing satis-
factorily. Lightly season the meat with salt
and pepper.

To make the stuffing, mix together the
breadcrumbs, bacon, olives, herbs and juice
and zest of the lemon. Bind together with the
egg. Divide the filling between the pieces of
rabbit, wrap round the meat and if necessary
secure with needle skewers or string. Arrange
the stuffed rabbit in a single layer in a cast-
iron casserole.

Make the marinade by mixing the tapenade with the lemon juice and olive oil.
Spoon over the rabbit, cover with a lid and
leave in a cold place for 4-8 hours.

Cook the rabbit in the same casserole, in
the preheated oven at the higher temperature
for 20 minutes and then at the lower temperature for 30 minutes or until the meat is
cooked right through. Serve with puréed or
creamed potatoes.

～

NAHE VALLEY-STYLE VENISON

This recipe came from friends who live in the wine-producing Nahe valley, a tributary of the Rhine. The venison is marinated in their local red wine – itself unusual in this white wine region of Germany – for 3-4 days before cooking, which produces tender meat with a splendid flavour.

SERVES 8-10

2-3 kg / 4½-7 lb joint of roasting venison

1 onion, peeled and finely chopped

1 clove garlic, peeled and chopped

1 tablespoon dark muscovado sugar

12 black peppercorns, crushed

¼ teaspoon ground cloves

3 tablespoons olive or sunflower oil

salt

300 ml / 10 fl oz red wine

300 ml / 10 fl oz beef or ham stock

BEURRE MANIÉ

1 tablespoon of butter blended with 1 tablespoon flour

OVEN

200°C 400°C Gas Mark 6 Roasting Oven

150°C 300°F Gas Mark 2 Simmering Oven

Place the venison in a large casserole or strong plastic bag in a bowl. Add the onion, garlic, sugar, peppercorns, cloves, oil, salt and wine and mix to distribute the marinade over the meat. Cover with a lid or seal the bag and refrigerate for 3-4 days, turning over the meat every day.

Lift the meat from the marinade and place in a lidded casserole, or a pot roaster. Spoon over half the marinade and cover with the lid. Roast in the hot preheated oven for 45 minutes. Spoon over more of the marinade and roast at the lower temperature for 2-3 hours or until a thick metal skewer penetrates the meat easily.

Transfer the venison to a carving board or plate, and keep warm for 20 minutes. Pour the stock into the roasting pan and simmer for 5 minutes, stirring with a wooden spoon to incorporate all the cooking juices. Just before serving add the *beurre manié* in small pieces whisking well to ensure the sauce is smooth. Pour into a warmed sauce boat and serve with the carved venison. Accompany with plain boiled noodles or creamed potatoes and SPICED PLUM SAUCE (see over), rowan, sloe or crab apple jelly.

VENISON SAUSAGES
BRAISED IN RED WINE

Venison sausages are traditionally braised in red wine. I devised this recipe to make the most of the fine sausages produced by Anne Petch's Heal Farm in North Devon.

SERVES 4-6

900 g / 2 lb venison and bacon sausages

30 g / 1 oz butter

1 shallot or ½ onion, peeled and chopped

1 clove of garlic, peeled and chopped

300 ml / 10 fl oz red wine

bouquet of fresh herbs – parsley, thyme, bay leaf, piece of celery

generous pinch of ground allspice

2 teaspoons potato flour

2 tablespoons redcurrant jelly

salt and freshly milled black pepper

1 tablespoon freshly chopped parsley or chives

OVEN
190°C 375°F Gas Mark 5 Roasting Oven

Cut the sausages into separate links. Melt the butter in a heavy-based frying-pan or skillet, add the shallot and garlic and cook for 2-3 minutes. Add the sausages and cook on all sides for 4-5 minutes. Pour the red wine into the pan, add the bouquet of herbs, celery and allspice and bring to the boil.

Transfer the pan contents to a preheated oven dish and cook for 15-20 minutes or until the sausages are cooked. Remove the herbs and transfer the sausages to a hot serving dish. Blend the potato flour with a tablespoon of cold water and stir into the oven dish with the redcurrant jelly. Stir the sauce

until it thickens. Season to taste, pour over the sausages and sprinkle the chopped parsley or chives on top. Serve with creamed potatoes.

SPICED PLUM SAUCE

An excellent sauce for roast duck and venison.

SERVES 8-10

340 g / 12 oz well-flavoured red plums

55 g / 2 oz light muscovado sugar

½ teaspoon ground cinnamon

good pinch of ground cloves and ground allspice

30 g / 1 oz butter, softened

OVEN
200°C 400°F Gas Mark 6 Roasting Oven

Halve the plums and remove the stones. Arrange the plums in an oven dish. Sprinkle the sugar and spices on top. Cook in the pre-heated oven for 15-20 minutes or until cooked.

Remove from the oven, cool slightly and then press through a fine sieve to make a smooth purée. Taste and if necessary add a little more sugar though the flavour should be a little sharp. If to be served hot, whisk in the butter until melted. Spoon into a hot dish and keep warm until ready to serve.

Right
VENISON SAUSAGES BRAISED
IN RED WINE

PHEASANT
COOKED WITH APPLES, CALVADOS AND CREAM

This classic dish of Normandy is unquestionably one of the best ways of cooking this sometimes dry game bird. Even my French friends admit that Scotch whisky makes a desirable alternative to Calvados in this recipe. Alternatively, you might be lucky enough to lay your hands on some Somerset apple spirit, our own equivalent to Calvados and a recent addition to the superb produce from the West Country.

SERVES 6-8

a brace of oven-ready pheasant

2 small peeled onions

the peel of a lemon

85 g / 3 oz Normandy butter

salt and milled black pepper

900 g / 2 lb Reinette or Cox's Orange Pippin apples, peeled, cored and thickly sliced

1 teaspoon *quatre épices* or ¼ teaspoon each of ground allspice and ground cinnamon

8 tablespoons Calvados

4 sprigs of thyme

400 ml / 14 fl oz *crème fraîche*

OVEN

200°C 400°F Gas Mark 6 Roasting Oven

325°C 160°F Gas Mark 3 Simmering Oven

Check that all stubs of feather have been removed from the pheasant. Place an onion and half the lemon peel inside each bird. Melt half the butter in a cast-iron casserole and brown the birds all over. Transfer to a plate and season well. Add the remaining butter to the casserole, add the apples and *quatre épices*. Stir to coat with butter and add half the Calvados. Make a nest in the middle of the apples in which to sit the pheasant. It may be easier to remove half the apple, place the pheasant on a bed of apple and arrange the rest of the slices over the birds. Add the sprigs of thyme and spoon half the *crème fraîche* on top. Cover with a tight-fitting lid.

Cook in a preheated oven for 30 minutes then lower the heat and cook for 30-40 minutes or until the pheasant is tender.

Transfer the pheasant to a hot serving dish and keep warm. Tilt the casserole and spoon the liquid into a pan. Boil fast until reduced by half. Add the remaining Calvados and *crème fraîche* and simmer again for several minutes until the flavour is mellowed and the liquid has the consistency of a sauce. Spoon the apples around each pheasant – leave whole or carved into portions – and pour over the sauce. Serve the dish with spinach or broccoli.

PHEASANT
BAKED WITH HAY

Using a terracotta chicken brick,
or a Romertopf casserole, to cook pheasant
normally produces rather more
succulent meat than when roasted. The
sweet-smelling hay in the recipe
imparts a delicious, almost smoky flavour
to the bird. And I enjoy the particular
appropriateness of the ingredients.

SERVES 2-4

1 or 2 oven-ready pheasant
sprigs of bay leaves
good knob of butter
few rashers of green streaky bacon
1-2 carrots, scrubbed and sliced
1 onion, peeled and sliced
4-6 tablespoons dry white wine
1-2 handfuls of fresh hay
GRAVY
150 ml/5 fl oz of full-bodied red wine
vegetable stock
1 small ripe tomato, quartered
bouquet of fresh herbs
salt and freshly milled pepper
BEURRE MANIÉ
½ teaspoon butter blended with ½ teaspoon
flour
1 teaspoon chopped parsley

OVEN

200°C 400°F Gas Mark 6 Roasting Oven

Soak the terracotta cooking pot covered in cold water for about 20 minutes until it has absorbed some of the water and feels quite heavy.

Meanwhile to make the gravy, extract any giblets from the pheasant and place in a small casserole with the red wine. Pour in vegetable stock to cover and add the tomato and the bouquet of herbs. Bring to the boil, cover and cook in the preheated oven for 45 minutes then strain into a pan.

Tuck the bay leaves inside the pheasant, spread the butter over the breast and place the bacon rashers on top. Make a layer of the sliced carrots and onion in the base of the pot, and add the white wine. Arrange the hay around the sides, sit the pheasant in the middle and cover with the lid. Cook in the preheated oven for 1 hour. Rest in a warm place for 15 minutes before removing the lid. Transfer the pheasant to a carving dish, keep warm and carefully spoon or pour off the surplus fat or strain the cooking juices into a gravy separator.

Pour the cooking juices, but not the fat, into the pan of giblet stock and boil fast for 5 minutes or so until the flavour is intensified. Season to taste and whisk in the *beurre manié* in small pieces, bringing back to the boil between pieces until the gravy is slightly thickened. Add the parsley, pour the gravy into a hot jug or gravy boat and serve with the carved pheasant.

Roast Partridge
with White Grapes

*Partridge with its fine, delicate flavour
is the king of game birds. One plump
bird makes a perfect meal for two.*

Serves 2

1 plump partridge

1 tangerine or small dessert apple

2 slices of unsmoked streaky bacon

55g / 2oz butter

salt and freshly milled pepper

115g / 4oz seedless white grapes, halved

150ml / 5fl oz full-bodied dry white wine

Oven
200°C 400°F Gas Mark 6 Roasting Oven

Place the partridge in a small roasting tin;
halve the tangerine or apple with their skins
and tuck it into the body cavity, and add the
rind of the bacon if you have it.

Spread half the butter over the breast and
legs of the bird and season. Stretch the
bacon, halved if necessary, over the bird and
press down on to the butter.

Roast in the preheated oven for 30 minutes
basting the bird with the buttery cooking
juices from time to time. Remove from the
oven, split the partridge in two through the
breast bone, discard the fruit and place the
halves on a hot serving dish. Cover with a
cloth and keep the meat warm while you
make the sauce.

Lightly sauté the grapes in the pan juices
and butter in the roasting pan for a few minutes. Add the wine and simmer together for
2-3 minutes. With a slotted spoon transfer the
grapes to the serving dish. Reduce the pan
sauce until slightly thickened. Taste and
adjust the seasoning accordingly. Remove the
pan from the heat and add the remaining
butter in small pieces. Shake the pan until
the butter has melted then spoon the sauce
over the partridge and serve. The HERB
POLENTA on p121 goes well with this dish.

Woodcock *sur Croute*

*The fine flavour of woodcock is a real treat
in this highly delicious French dish.*

Serves 2

15g / ½oz butter

1 undrawn woodcock, oven-ready

salt and freshly milled black pepper

1 slim shallot, peeled and finely chopped

a sprig of thyme

2 tablespoons dry white wine

1 chicken or duck liver, lightly cooked, or
1 tablespoon pâté

1-2 teaspoons olive oil

½ teaspoon white wine vinegar

a little Dijon mustard

½ teaspoon chopped parsley

a few drops of cognac

2 slices of bread, freshly toasted

Oven
200°C 400°F Gas Mark 6 Roasting Oven

Melt the butter in a small, lidded casserole
and lightly brown the woodcock over moderate heat for 6-8 minutes. Turn the bird on its

back and season with salt and pepper. Add the shallot, thyme and wine to the pan.

Cover tightly and cook in the preheated oven for 40-50 minutes or until the flesh on the leg is cooked. Spoon off any surplus fat and discard the thyme.

In a bowl or mortar, pound the liver or pâté with the olive oil, vinegar, mustard, parsley and brandy. Use poultry shears to halve the bird, scrape the trail (the dark purée) from inside the bird into the casserole and stir in the liver mixture and heat gently.

Cut the pieces of toast to the same size as the woodcock. Spread each piece with the hot purée and place the woodcock on top. Serve straight away.

~

ROAST GUINEA FOWL WITH PORT WINE AND CHERRY SAUCE

For the best flavour use sharply-sweet morello cherries for this sauce which also goes well with roast quail or roast duckling.

SERVES 4

900 g-1.4 kg / 2-3 lb oven-ready guinea fowl
100 g / 3½ oz butter
6 juniper berries, bruised
bouquet of fresh herbs – parsley, thyme and bay leaves
salt and freshly milled pepper

SAUCE

1 shallot, peeled and finely chopped
225 g / 8 oz ripe morello cherries, pitted
½ teaspoon finely grated zest of orange
55 ml / 2 fl oz ruby port
115 g / 4 oz redcurrant jelly
¼ teaspoon finely chopped lemon thyme (if available)

OVEN

190°C 375°F Gas Mark 5 Roasting Oven

Place the guinea fowl in a lightly buttered roasting pan. Remove any giblets from the guinea fowl and reserve for making gravy. Tuck the juniper berries and bouquet of herbs inside the guinea fowl. Spread half the butter over the skin of the bird, making a thicker layer over the breast meat. Season with salt and pepper and press buttered paper over the bird.

Roast in the preheated oven allowing 20 minutes per 450 g / 1 lb and 20 minutes over. As with all poultry the meat is cooked when the juices from the leg joint run clear. When the bird is cooked, transfer to a warm place for 20 minutes before carving.

To make the sauce, cook the shallot in the remaining butter for 3-4 minutes until soft but not coloured. Add the cherries and any juice, with the orange zest, port and redcurrant jelly. Stir and bring to the boil then turn down the heat and simmer for 20 minutes until the cherries are cooked and the liquid has reduced to a slightly syrupy sauce. Stir in the lemon thyme.

Pour off the fat from the roasting tin and stir 1-2 tablespoons of the cooking juices into the cherry sauce. Season the sauce to taste and, if appropriate, add an extra splash of port. Spoon the sauce into a jug and serve with the carved guinea fowl.

~

GUINEA FOWL
WITH HONEY AND QUINCE

In our village, quinces grow almost as profusely as cider apples. Their lovely scented flavour complements guinea fowl beautifully.

SERVES 4

1.5 kg / 3½ lb oven-ready guinea fowl

1 large ripe quince

2 Cox's Orange Pippin apples

2 bay leaves

2 sprigs thyme

55 g / 2 oz butter

2-3 tablespoons honey

½ teaspoon chopped lemon verbena leaves

2 tablespoons thick cream (optional)

200 ml / 7 fl oz dry cider

100 ml / 3½ fl oz vegetable stock

salt

pinch of ground allspice

OVEN
200°C 400°F Gas Mark 6 Roasting Oven

Place the guinea fowl in a roasting tin. Tuck the peelings of both the quince and apples into the body cavity with the bay leaves and fresh thyme and spread half the butter over the breast of the bird and then cover with buttered paper.

Roast in the preheated oven for 1-1½ hours or until the juice from the leg runs clear. Meanwhile quarter the quince and the apples and core the fruit. Cut into small pieces and place in a casserole with the butter, honey and 3 tablespoons of water. Cook in the oven alongside the guinea fowl for 30-40 minutes or until tender. Stir in the lemon verbena and the cream and keep warm.

Transfer the guinea fowl to a carving board or plate and keep warm. If neccesary, once again, pour the fat from the roasting tin. Add the cider and vegetable stock and stir over moderate heat to incorporate the cooking juices. Bring to the boil and cook until reduced by half. Season to taste with salt and allspice and pour into a gravy boat and serve with the carved guinea fowl and the honey and quince sauce.

QUAILS
WITH ANGEL'S WINGS

The fanciful title of this dish was given by a friend for whom I devised it. Small quails are wrapped in Florence fennel so that the vegetable resembles tiny wings.

SERVES 4

4 oven-ready quails

2 large heads of Florence fennel

55 g / 2 oz butter, softened

a few fronds of fennel – either from the stalk of the vegetable or of the herb, finely chopped

1 tablespoon finely chopped parsley

squeeze of lemon juice

4 fresh bay leaves

salt and freshly milled pepper

3-4 tablespoons Pernod

150 ml / 5 fl oz *crème fraîche*

OVEN
190°C 375°F Gas Mark 5 Roasting Oven

Wipe the quails with a kitchen paper and set aside – quails from France sometimes have their heads intact, I usually remove them and give them to the cats.

Trim the top and bottom of each head of fennel so that you can detach two of the largest pieces from each. Do this carefully without splitting them. Blanch the fennel in boiling water for 1-2 minutes, then drain on kitchen paper. Use the rest of the fennel in a salad or another dish.

Blend half the butter with the chopped fronds of fennel, the parsley and some lemon juice. Melt the remaining butter in a flame-proof casserole and lightly brown the quail all over. Lift out the quail and place a tea-spoon of the savoury butter inside each bird, then tuck in a bay leaf. Spread some butter over the breasts of the quails and enclose each in a layer of fennel so that the corners look like the edge of a cloak over each breast. Lightly season each bird with salt and pepper and place in the casserole. Spinkle the Pernod over them and cover with buttered paper and a lid.

Cook in the preheated oven for 30-40 min-utes until the meat is cooked. Transfer the quail and fennel to a hot serving dish and keep warm. Add 2 tablespoons of Pernod to the juices in the casserole and simmer for 1-2 minutes. Stir in the *crème fraîche* and when hot, add any remaining herb butter. Taste and, if necesssary, season further and add just a spot of Pernod, though the sauce should only hint at the aniseed flavour of the wine, simply to echo the flavour of the fen-nel. Spoon the sauce over the quail and serve straight away.

QUAIL COOKED IN VINE LEAVES WITH PESTO

Quails are under-appreciated in Britain, yet their subtle flavour and very tender flesh is highly popular in France, where the birds are widely farmed and sold in supermarkets.

SERVES 2-4

8-12 vine leaves, fresh and blanched or brined and rinsed

4 oven-ready quail

pesto (see p56)

1 tablespoon olive oil

OVEN
190°C 375°F Gas Mark 5 Roasting Oven

Place 2-3 vine leaves in a lightly oiled, large cast-iron *gratin* dish. Spread pesto over the body of one quail, place on the vine leaves and wrap them round to enclose the bird. Repeat with the other quail and place beside each other in the dish – alternatively place each on a separate *gratin* dish. Brush the vine leaf parcels with olive oil.

Roast the quail in the preheated oven for 30-40 minutes or until cooked. Serve with SAFFRON ORZO (p56).

BREASTS OF WOOD PIGEON WITH CEPS AND PUFF PASTRY

This is an attractive first course or light supper dish. The meatiest part of a wood pigeon is the breast, use the remaining carcases for making stock. If using dried wild mushrooms, soak them in a little warm white wine and use the liquid to replace some of the stock.

SERVES 4

85 g / 3 oz prepared-weight puff pastry
egg yolk
the breast meat of 2 young wood pigeons
salt and milled pepper
30 g / 1 oz butter
1 shallot, peeled and finely chopped
2 slices smoked streaky bacon, diced
115 g / 4 oz ceps, *porcini* or other wild
mushrooms, thickly sliced
150 ml / 5 fl oz red wine
150 ml / 5 fl oz stock
2 tablespoons *crème fraîche*

OVEN

200°C 400°F Gas Mark 6 Roasting Oven

Roll out the pastry into a 20 × 12 cm / 8 × 5 in rectangle. Trim the edges straight and cut into 4 rectangles. Brush the pastry with the egg yolk and decorate with a few leaves and berries made from the trimmings. Transfer the pastry to a non-stick baking sheet and chill for 15 minutes. Bake in the preheated oven for 10-15 minutes until well-risen and golden brown. Cool the pastry on wire rack and reheat in a hot oven for 2-3 minutes when ready to serve.

Slice the pigeon breast meat thinly and season lightly. Melt the butter in a pan and cook the shallot and bacon until starting to colour. Add the wood pigeon and sauté for only 2-3 minutes, add the ceps and when cooked transfer the contents of the pan to a hot dish and keep warm. Pour the wine and the stock into the pan and bring to the boil, stirring well to incorporate all the pan juices. Reduce over high heat by about half, return the pigeon mixture to the sauce and stir in the *crème fraîche*. Heat through and check the seasoning.

Slice each piece of puff pastry in 2, place the bottom halves on individual warmed plates. Spoon over the pigeon mixture and cover with the pastry lids. Serve straight away.

∼

Right
BREASTS OF WOOD PIGEON WITH
CEPS AND PUFF PASTRY

WILD DUCK
WITH GIN AND JUNIPER BERRIES

Wild duck has a particular affinity with juniper berries, as they are naturally, or when providing the main flavouring in gin.

SERVES 2-3

680-900 g / 1½-2 lb oven-ready wild duck or mallard

1 carrot, 1 small onion, 1 stick of celery, all roughly chopped

18 juniper berries

1 bay leaf

sprig of thyme

salt

150 ml / 5 fl oz good vegetable or jellied chicken stock

55-85 ml / 2-3 fl oz gin

55 g / 2 oz butter

GARNISH

watercress

OVEN

200°C 400°F Gas Mark 6 Roasting Oven

Place the duck, with the giblets if you have them, and the chopped vegetables in a roasting tin. Crush half the juniper berries and place in the cavity of the duck with the bay leaf and the sprig of thyme. Sprinkle salt over the skin of the duck and roast in the preheated oven for 45 minutes. Pour off any surplus fat from the roasting tin and turn over the duck so that it is breast side down. Roast for 10 minutes and then, if the duck is sufficiently cooked, transfer to a hot serving dish and keep warm.

Pour off the fat from the roasting tin and add the remaining juniper berries and the stock (to make jellied stock boil fast over a high heat to reduce). Boil fast for 5 minutes, stirring the pan to incorporate all the cooking juices. Pour the contents of the pan into a sieve and press with a wooden spoon to release all the flavours from the vegetables and giblets.

Pour the gin into the pan and set light to it. Return the strained juices to the pan and simmer for 2 minutes, stirring all the time. Remove from the heat and add the butter in small pieces, shaking the pan until the butter has thickened the sauce. Pour into a small hot jug or sauceboat and serve with the carved duck.

RAISED GAME PIE

This is a magnificent pie for a special occasion. A raised pie can be made 1-3 days in advance provided that it is wrapped carefully in greaseproof paper and a cloth and is kept in a refrigerator or a cold store.

SERVES 8-10

JELLIED STOCK

1 pig's trotter, halved

1 small onion, chopped

1 carrot, chopped

1 stick of celery, chopped

1 bay leaf

1 bouquet garni of fresh herbs

salt and freshly milled pepper

FILLING

900 g / 2 lb raw, boneless game meat, e.g. a mixture of pheasant, wild duck, hare, pigeon (combined with some turkey, chicken or guinea fowl, if preferred)

225 g / 8 oz smoked streaky bacon, diced

115 g / 4 oz mushrooms, sliced

2 tablespoons parsley, chopped

½ teaspoon ground mace

150 ml / 5 fl oz port or red wine

HOT WATER CRUST PASTRY

450 g / 1 lb plain flour

2 teaspoons salt

150 g / 5 oz clarified dripping or lard

150 ml / 5 fl oz milk

egg yolk to glaze

OVEN

200°C 400°F Gas Mark 6 Roasting Oven

180°C 350°F Gas Mark 4 Baking Oven

Make the jellied stock by simmering (on the hob or in the oven) the pig's trotter with the vegetables and herbs, and enough water to cover, for 1-2 hours in a covered pan. Strain and return the liquid to the pan, boil fast over high heat to reduce to about 300 ml/ 10 fl oz. Remove from the heat, season to taste and set aside.

Prepare the pie filling by cutting the game into 1 cm/½ in pieces. Mix with the bacon, mushrooms, parsley, wine, and salt and pepper. Butter a hinged metal pie tin or a loose-bottomed 25 cm/10 in diameter cake tin. Make the hot water crust pastry by sieving the flour and salt into a mixing bowl. Melt the fat in a pan with the milk and 150 ml/ 5 fl oz water and heat to body temperature/98°F. Pour on to the flour and mix well with a wooden spoon. Knead the dough in the bowl until smooth. Roll out two-thirds of the pastry to line the base and sides of the pie tin. Spoon in the meat filling. Then roll out the remaining pastry to make a lid. Cut to fit (keep the trimmings for the decoration) then brush the pastry edges with water and squeeze the joints firmly together. Make 3-4 steam vents in the lid and position a roll of foil or baking paper in one to prevent it from closing during baking. Decorate the lid of the pie with pastry leaves and berries, and brush the lid with egg yolk.

Bake in a preheated oven at the higher temperature for 30 minutes. Then lower the temperature and bake for a further 2 hours. Remove the pie from the oven, cool for 20 minutes then pour the jellied stock into the pie (use the small foil roll in the steam vent as a funnel). Leave the pie to cool in a cold place and remove from the tin when ready to serve.

CHAPTER 6

EGGS
AND
CHEESE

~

*Here in Devon, we can choose from our
own home-produced supply of
fresh and mature cheeses made from the
milk of cows, ewes and goats and
superlative free-range eggs; a galaxy of
glorious West Country ingredients
representing English country food
at its best.*

Left
HUNGARIAN *LECSO*
WITH BAKED EGGS *page 111*

I N NATURE eggs are a seasonal occurrence. When fowl are reared properly, with hens free to forage and scratch for food in a grassy orchard or meadow, pullets begin to lay as the days lengthen and the sun shines more brightly during early spring. Left to themselves, and without the stimulus of artificial light, hens lay fewer eggs during the dark winter months. Hence the old methods of preserving eggs to maintain a supply of this valuable food while the hens were resting. I remember my mother and grandmother preserving raw eggs in isinglass, while hard-boiled eggs were pickled in brine or seasoned vinegar.

There is, though, nothing to equal the flavour of a warm, new-laid and truly free-range egg. It can't be faked or substituted. The glowing yolk has a viscosity never found in an old egg, the white is pearly and when perfectly cooked has a delicately crêpe-like texture with no hint of rubbery toughness. How tragic that this simple, good country food – which is not difficult to produce from happy hens that enjoy the freedom nature intended – has become for many people as rare as caviare.

A really fresh egg is a most nutritious food; lightly boiled it is often our first solid nourishment. When a little older we appreciate baked eggs, *oeufs sur le plat*, which taste superb, are uniquely satisfying and easy enough for anyone to prepare. Simply melt some unsalted butter in an oven dish, break fresh eggs into the dish and season lightly with salt and pepper. Then bake the eggs in a preheated oven for 5 minutes or so until the whites are set and the yolks are still liquid. Serve straight away with warm crusty bread and butter.

Cheese – with just a few exceptions – has a most obliging property in cooking, it melts. Sliced or shaved thinly and arranged on buttered toast or grated over cooked food and placed in a hot oven, cheese melts deliciously to make an instant and appetizing sauce.

Wherever you live in the country it makes good sense and displays a proper regional pride to buy your local cheeses and discover their particular qualities: which cheese goes well with a dessert pear, or a stick of crisp celery, or a sliver of Florence fennel; which cheese is best for toasting; and which cheese imparts a fine flavour to a sauce.

BEENLEIGH BLUE CHEESE SAUCE

A good local cheese sauce is an essential element in country cooking. Serve with vegetables, pasta, grilled chicken and smoked white fish and vary its flavour by adding a few finely chopped herbs such as parsley, chives or oregano. By cooking the sauce slowly in the oven, it develops a velvet smoothness and delicate mellow flavour.

MAKES APPROXIMATELY
500 ML / 18 FL OZ

30 g / 1 oz butter
¼ small shallot, peeled and finely chopped
20 g / ¾ oz plain white flour
425 ml / 15 fl oz whole milk
55 g / 2 oz Beenleigh Blue sheep's milk cheese
(or similar), chopped
freshly grated nutmeg
1 bay leaf

OVEN
120°C 250°F Gas Mark ½ Simmering Oven

Melt the butter in a cast-iron casserole and stir in the shallot for 1 minute, not allowing it to colour. Stir in the flour for 1 minute then gradually whisk in the milk, using a balloon whisk. Add the cheese and cook, whisking all the time, for 2 minutes until the mixture thickens slightly. Season with nutmeg – the cheese usually provides sufficient salt – add the bay leaf and cover with a tight-fitting lid.

Place the casserole on a folded newspaper in a roasting tin of warm water and cook in the preheated oven for 1 hour. Remove the bay leaf, stir the cheese sauce and keep warm until needed.

~

WILD MUSHROOM SOUFFLE

In a soufflé, the intense flavour of dried wild mushrooms, such as porcini *or ceps, has much to commend it, furthermore they are available all year around. This recipe can be made with fresh wild mushrooms – 1-2 handfuls will give a good flavour – if you first cook them in butter over high heat until they have surrendered most of their liquid. Then blend them with the cream and continue the method from the second paragraph.*

SERVES 2-4

10 g / ¼ oz dried wild mushrooms - *porcini* or ceps

150 ml / 5 fl oz single cream, warmed

small clove garlic, peeled and crushed

20 g / ¾ oz butter

15 g / ½ oz flour

2 egg yolks

good pinch of freshly grated nutmeg

good pinch of ground mace

salt

3 egg whites

OVEN

220°C 425°F Gas Mark 7 Roasting Oven

Use scissors to snip the dried mushrooms into small pieces and stir into the cream with the crushed garlic. Set aside in a warm place for at least 30 minutes or until the fungi have softened and the cream has absorbed their intense flavour.

Melt the butter in a small pan, stir in the flour and cook for 1 minute not allowing it to colour. Off the heat gradually add the mushroom cream, stirring all the time until the mixture is smooth and thick. Remove from the heat and beat in the egg yolks with the nutmeg, mace and salt to taste.

Whisk the egg whites until stiff then fold into the mushroom mixture. Spoon the mixture into one buttered 600 ml / 1 pint or 4 200 ml / 7 fl oz individual soufflé dishes. Smooth the top level and place the dish(es) on a baking sheet. Cook in the preheated oven for 12-15 minutes for the larger soufflé or only 8-10 minutes for the smaller ones. Serve straight from the oven, when the soufflés should be golden brown and well-risen but still almost liquid in the centre.

An excellent variation is to half-fill the soufflé dish, then spoon in some dressed crab meat or a few pieces of mature *chèvre* (goats' milk cheese). Cover with the rest of the mixture and cook as above.

~

TERRINE OF COURGETTES WITH TARRAGON

*My local restaurant in Montelimar
serves this terrine of sliced courgettes set in a
tarragon-flavoured custard (tarragon
goes well with much summer food). Serve,
cut in slices, as a separate course or as
an accompanying vegetable dish.*

SERVES 4-6

3 large eggs

12 tarragon leaves, chopped

½ slim clove of garlic, peeled and crushed or
finely chopped

450 g / 1 lb slim young courgettes

salt

knob of butter

200 ml / 7 fl oz *crème fraîche* or double cream

freshly milled pepper

OVEN

200°C 400°F Gas Mark 6 Roasting Oven

Lightly whisk the eggs with the tarragon and
garlic and set aside for the herbs to perfume
the mixture.

Slice the courgettes, sprinkle lightly with
salt and leave in a colander set over a plate
for 20 minutes for some of the liquid to be
shed. Rinse the courgettes in cold water,
drain well and dry on a clean tea-cloth or
kitchen paper. Rub the butter over the inside
of a 1.3 litre / 2¼ pint cast-iron or Pyrex terrine dish and add the sliced courgettes in layers. Whisk the *crème fraîche* into the egg
mixture and season with pepper. Pour the
egg mixture over the courgettes and cover
the dish with buttered paper.

Place the terrine in a roasting pan of warm
water to make a bain-marie and cook in the
preheated oven for about 45 minutes until
the custard is set. Remove from the oven and
allow to cool slightly before serving, then cut
into slices with a very sharp knife.

COCOTTE EGGS WITH SORREL PUREE

*A dish I never tire of, new-laid
eggs baked with cream and garden herbs
constitutes a perfect marriage.
If need be, cocotte eggs can be cooked on the
hob: place the cocotte dishes in a
pan of shallow simmering water, cover with
a lid or a hood of foil and cook
until the eggs are set.*

SERVES 2-4

100 g / 3½ oz sorrel leaves

55 g / 2 oz butter

slim clove of garlic, peeled and crushed

salt to taste

4 large new-laid eggs

milled black pepper

4 tablespoons *crème fraîche* or double cream

1 teaspoon chopped chives and chervil

OVEN

180°C 350°F Gas Mark 4 Roasting Oven

Wash the sorrel and drain in a colander, strip
the stems from the leaves and discard. Melt

the butter in a small pan, add the garlic and sorrel and cook over moderate heat, stirring all the time for 3-5 minutes until you have a small amount of olive-green purée and all surplus water has evaporated. Season to taste with salt. If need be, the cooked sorrel purée can be cooled and then stored in a small lidded container in the refrigerator for up to 48 hours.

Divide the purée between 4 90 ml / 3 fl oz buttered cocotte dishes. Break an egg into each and season with salt and pepper. Add a spoonful of *crème fraîche* to each dish and sprinkle with chives and chervil. Bake for 8-12 minutes or until the white of egg is set and the yolk is still liquid. Serve straight away with fresh bread.

~

HUNGARIAN *LECSO* ## WITH BAKED EGGS

Sweet peppers cooked in the Hungarian style with bacon and paprika make an aromatic and satisfying sauce for noodles or, as in this recipe, for baked eggs.
There is an equally fine Spanish version of this egg dish where the paprika and some of the sweet peppers are replaced by a handful of cooked green beans, a few blanched garden peas and a splash of fino sherry.

SERVES 4

1 tablespoon sunflower oil
2 slices smoked streaky bacon, diced
1 large onion, peeled and chopped
2 teaspoons sweet paprika
1 teaspoon hot paprika
225 g / 8 oz ripe tomatoes, chopped
3-4 red sweet peppers, deseeded and sliced
3-4 yellow or green sweet peppers, deseeded and sliced
salt and cayenne pepper
4-8 eggs

OVEN
200°C 400°F Gas Mark 6 Roasting Oven

Heat the oil in a large, shallow skillet or frying-pan. Cook the bacon and onion for 5-6 minutes until softened but not coloured. Stir in the two kinds of paprika and cook for 2 minutes. Add the tomatoes and as they begin to soften, add the sliced sweet peppers. Season with salt and stir. Transfer to the preheated oven and cook for 20-30 minutes or until the peppers have softened and cooked to an almost chutney consistency.

Remove the pan of *lecso* from the oven and use the back of a spoon to make a depression for each egg. Carefully break an egg into each depression and season with a little salt and cayenne pepper. Cover the pan with a hood of foil and replace in the oven for 5-6 minutes or until the whites of egg are set. Serve straight away with warm bread.

~

Roasted Radicchio
with Dolcelatte Cheese

*An Italian dish that is so well-flavoured that
it can be served as a separate sauce.*

Serves 6

6 heads of young round-leaved radicchio
di Verona
85 g / 3 oz butter
170 g / 6 oz Dolcelatte or Gorgonzola, diced
2 tablespoons balsamic or red wine vinegar
1 tablespoon chives, finely chopped
freshly milled black pepper

Oven
200°C 400°F Gas Mark 6 Roasting Oven

Trim the base of each head of radicchio and
remove any damaged leaves. Cut each head
in half lengthwise. Melt three-quarters of the
butter in a cast-iron skillet large enough to
hold the radicchio in a single layer. When
foaming add the radicchio cut side down,
and spoon over some of the butter to coat
the vegetable. Cover with buttered paper and
cook in the preheated oven for 8-10 minutes.

Turn each piece of radicchio cut side up
and sprinkle on cheese. Replace in the oven
for 4-5 minutes until the cheese has melted.

Transfer the radicchio to a hot serving dish
or individual plates. Add the vinegar and the
chives to the pan and stir to incorporate the
cooking juices. Remove from the heat and
add the remaining butter, shake until melted
and spoon over the radicchio. Season with
pepper and serve straight away while hot.

≈

Smoked Cheese Potato Cake

*An English smoked cheese like Oak Smoked
Cheddar from Quicke's Farm in
Devon goes well in this classic potato dish
from the Loire valley.*

Serves 6

55 g / 2 oz unsalted butter
1 slim clove of garlic, peeled and crushed
900 g / 2 lb waxy potatoes (like Desirée), peeled
and sliced
170 g / 6 oz smoked Cheddar cheese, thinly sliced
freshly grated nutmeg
salt
Garnish
1 teaspoon parsley, finely chopped

Oven
190°C 375°F Gas Mark 5 Roasting Oven

Spread half the butter over the inside of a
non-stick 18 cm / 7 in cake tin or a *Pommes
Anna* mould. Sprinkle some garlic over the
base and arrange alternate layers of potato
and cheese on top, seasoning with nutmeg,
salt and the garlic. Use cheese for the top
layer. Dot with the remaining butter and place
a close-fitting lid or baking sheet over the tin.

Bake in the preheated oven for 50-60 minutes or until the potato is cooked. Run the
blade of a knife around the edge of the
cake and turn out on to a hot serving dish.
Sprinkle over the chopped parsley and serve.

≈

Right
Smoked Cheese Potato Cake

Spinach, Artichoke and Goats' Cheese Filo Pie

A paper-thin pastry case containing creamy cheese and vegetables that can be served as a vegetarian main course.

Serves 6-8

FILLING
225 g / 8 oz fresh young spinach leaves

225 g / 8 oz medium-fat curd cheese

2 eggs, size 3

salt

freshly grated nutmeg

140 g / 5 oz soft goats' cheese

80 ml / 3 fl oz soured cream

¼ teaspoon ground coriander seeds

freshly grated black pepper

PIE
6 sheets 20 × 10 cm / 16 × 8 in filo pastry

30 g / 1 oz butter, melted

6-8 artichoke hearts, sliced – either freshly cooked or tinned and drained

OVEN
200°C 400°F Gas Mark 6 Roasting Oven

Make the filling by washing the spinach leaves. Cook in the water adhering to the leaves for 3-5 minutes, drain well and place in a food processor. Add the curd cheese and one egg, then process until finely chopped. Season to taste with salt and nutmeg. In a separate bowl, blend the goats' cheese with the remaining egg, the soured cream and the coriander. Season to taste with black pepper.

Pile the filo pastry sheets on a flat surface and keep covered. Brush the top one with butter and place in a buttered 25 cm / 10 in diameter loose-bottomed cake tin. Gently press the pastry across the base and up the side of the tin, leaving the surplus to drape over the rim. Repeat the process with another three sheets of pastry, overlapping each one so that the tin is lined with pastry all round. Spoon the spinach filling into the pastry case, arrange the sliced artichoke hearts on top, then spoon over the goats' cheese mixture.

Brush the filo pastry sheets with butter and gently crumple on top of the filling to resemble crinkled paper. Fold in the surplus pastry from the rim in the same way. Place the pie on a baking sheet and bake in a preheated oven for 30-40 minutes until the pastry is golden and crisp and the filling is set. Remove from the oven and allow to cool slightly before removing from the cake tin. Serve in wedges with a salad of curly endive.

~

Stilton and Sesame Straws

Home-made cheese straws are one of life's small luxuries.

MAKES ABOUT 50 BISCUITS
115 g / 4 oz plain flour

½ teaspoon cayenne pepper

115 g / 4 oz butter

55 g / 2 oz Stilton cheese, crumbled

1 egg yolk

2 tablespoons toasted sesame seeds

2 tablespoons coarse sea salt

OVEN
190°C 375°F Gas Mark 5 roasting or baking oven

Sift the flour and cayenne pepper. Rub in the butter, work in the cheese and knead into a ball. Wrap and chill for 30 minutes.

Roll out the dough on a floured board until 3 mm/⅛ in thickness. Brush with the egg yolk and sprinkle with sesame seeds and sea salt. Cut into narrow strips.

Transfer to a buttered baking sheet and bake in a preheated oven for 10-15 minutes until golden and crisp. Cool on a wire rack.

ALMOND AND CHIVE SABLE BISCUITS

Serve these light, crisp biscuits with a subtly flavoured soup or to accompany drinks.

MAKES 24 - 30 BISCUITS
70 g / 2½ oz unsalted butter, softened
1 teaspoon finely chopped chives
140 g / 5 oz plain white flour
30 g / 1 oz ground almonds
30 g / 1 oz freshly grated Parmesan cheese
1 egg yolk mixed with 1 tablespoon water
30 g / 1 oz split, blanched almonds

OVEN
180°C 350°F Gas Mark 4 Baking Oven

Cream the butter with the chives. Sift the flour and ground almonds and stir in the Parmesan cheese. Rub in the chive butter and mix to a dough with the egg yolk and water. You may need to add a little extra water.

Take a teaspoon of the dough and gently roll into a ball on a lightly floured surface.

Slightly flatten into an oval shape on a buttered baking sheet and press a split almond on top. Make the remaining biscuits in the same way.

Bake in the preheated oven for 15-20 minutes or until the biscuits are golden and crisp. Cool on the tray for 2 minutes then transfer to a cloth-lined plate and serve.

PARMESAN PUFFS

Quickly-baked cheese choux pastry tastes at its best straight from the oven.

MAKES ABOUT 20 BISCUITS
55 g / 2 oz butter
100 g / 3½ oz plain flour, sieved
2 eggs, size 2, beaten
30 g / 1 oz Parmesan cheese, finely grated
salt and cayenne pepper

OVEN
220°F 425°F Gas Mark 7 Roasting Oven

Melt the butter in a pan with 150 ml / 5 fl oz water and bring to the boil. Remove from the heat and add the flour all at once. Beat the mixture until it is smooth and forms a ball. Add the eggs, a little at a time, beating well after each addition. Finally mix in the cheese and seasoning to taste.

Place teaspoons of the mixture on a buttered non-stick baking sheet and bake in a preheated oven for 10-12 minutes until well puffed up and golden brown. Serve hot.

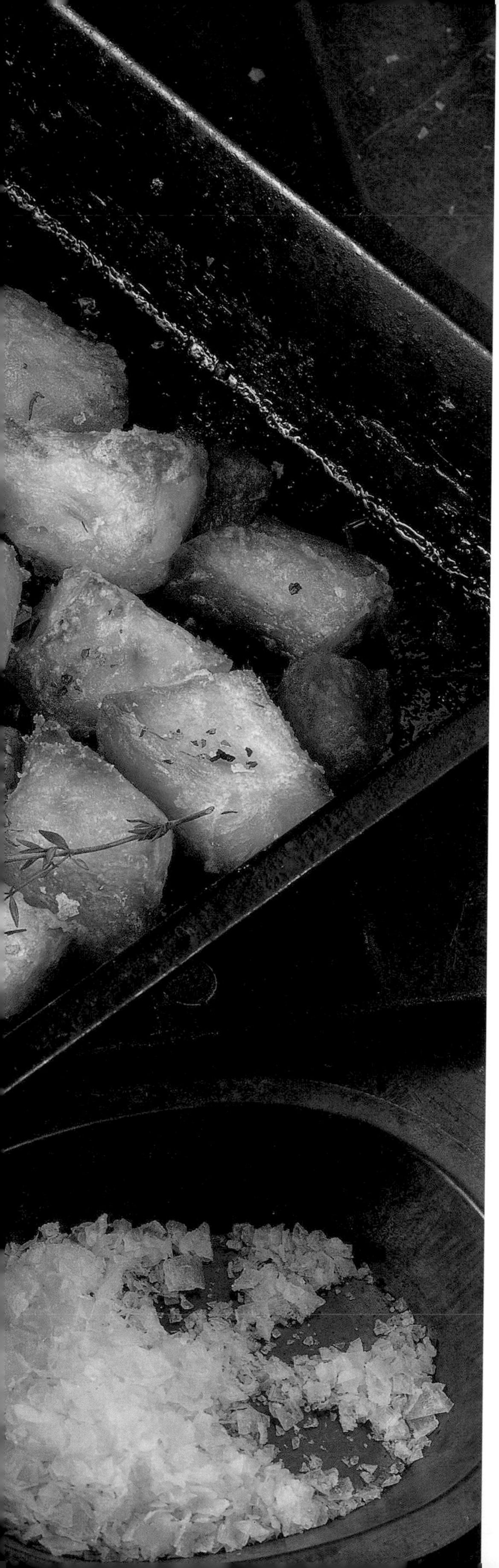

CHAPTER 7

VEGETABLES AND SALADS

One of the great pleasures of living in the country is to be able to gather one's own food. A basket of vegetables, herbs and fruit newly picked from the garden is a harvest of the finest ingredients anyone could wish for.

Left
OVEN-ROASTED FRENCH FRIES
page 119

Spinach and sorrel, tomatoes and beans, strawberries, apples and pears, artichokes and fennel, no matter that they are not all the same size and one or two may have been nibbled by insects, this is the most beautiful food one can eat; pure, undefiled by chemicals and sprays, the produce shimmering with its bloom of freshness. It is the just reward for one's care and effort, the result of living in harmony with the natural world.

When it comes to cooking such superlative produce, I prefer to prepare it with the utmost simplicity. It's too easy to dominate one's ingredients in cooking, subjecting them to one's will, or flattering one's ego with unnecessarily complicated recipes, when letting well alone is often the wisest and most delicious course of action.

If you wash and scrub a large, handsome potato, dry it and prick the skin all over, and bake it in a hot oven for an hour or so, you will produce one of the finest dishes it is possible to eat. Cut the potato in half and cover with shavings of cool, sweet butter, or douse it with the best olive oil, and add flakes of sea salt and some crushed black pepper. Could anyone not enjoy such perfect food?

Sometimes, I slice the scrubbed raw potato and in a small ovenproof dish, arrange layers of potato, each scattered with crushed garlic and slivers of Stilton cheese. Spoon over a little thick cream and bake until cooked, to produce a simple appetizing meal.

Or a crisp, sweet-flavoured cabbage – the most unjustly treated of our native vegetables – shredded and then braised in a hot oven with diced shallot and smoked bacon, sprigs of fresh thyme and a splash of red wine, makes a superb winter dish. Thyme is a powerful herb and should be used with discretion. And small spring turnips, simply washed and baked whole in a covered dish, with some butter, a scrap of garlic and the juice and zest of an orange, until glazed and aromatic. And a summer picking of bright green garden peas cooked with rice in chicken broth are unforgettably good.

In these days when a freshly-pulled carrot still damp from the earth has become a luxury food, the centuries-old advice of such pastoral prophets as Thomas Tusser, John Evelyn and William Cobbett has never been more timely; their advocacy of simple home-grown food is a sane antidote to the threat to rural life of twentieth-century industrialization.

Oven-roasted French Fries

For a crisp, golden finish to these irresistible potatoes, reserve any duck or goose fat you have or use grapeseed oil – olive oil doesn't work so well.

S E R V E S 4

900 g / 2 lb waxy potatoes like Desirée
salt
4 tablespoons grapeseed oil or duck or goose fat
30 g / 1 oz unsalted butter
herbes de Provence or caraway seeds
sea salt flakes

O V E N
200°C 400°F Gas Mark 6 Roasting Oven

Peel the potatoes and cut into neat walnut-size pieces. Cook in boiling salted water for 6-8 minutes until just tender. Drain and then replace the pan over the hob to drive off any surplus water.

Meanwhile heat the oil and butter in a roasting tin in the preheated oven. Add the drained potatoes and spoon the fat over them until evenly coated. Roast in the oven for 20-30 minutes until golden and crisp. Halfway through the cooking time sprinkle the herbs or caraway seeds over the potatoes. Pour off the roasting fat, drain the potatoes on kitchen paper and transfer to a hot serving dish. Sprinkle with flakes of sea salt and serve straight away.

Fondant Potatoes

Small new potatoes cooked just in butter until golden and crisp are an early summer treat.

S E R V E S 4

680 g / 1½ lb baby new potatoes
100 g / 3½ oz clarified butter
Maldon sea salt flakes

O V E N
190°C 375°F Gas Mark 5
Roasting or Baking Oven

Scrape the potatoes, rinse in cold water and dry them in a tea-towel. Melt the butter in a wide, heavy-based pan – like a lidded cast-iron casserole. Add the potatoes and shake over moderate heat until they are coated with butter. Cover with a tight-fitting lid and cook in the preheated oven or over low heat for 20-30 minutes. it is important to shake the pan now and again to prevent the potatoes from sticking to the base.

When the potatoes are cooked, remove the lid and sauté them briefly over high heat to drive off any moisture and to give them a crisp finish. Transfer the potatoes to a hot serving dish and sprinkle with salt. Serve straight away.

POTATO PUREE
WITH GARLIC AND OLIVE OIL

The best olive oil, juicy fat-cloved garlic and well-flavoured fluffy potatoes utterly transform this scrumptious variation on familar creamed potatoes. Well made, it's a dish good enough to eat on on its own, or partner with big meaty sausages or thick rashers of smoked bacon and field mushrooms.

S E R V E S   2 - 4

900 g / 2 lb fluffy mashing potatoes

½ teaspoon salt

4-6 fat cloves of garlic, peeled and sliced

6 tablespoons fruity extra virgin olive oil

1 teaspoon thyme leaves, coarsely chopped

milled black pepper and sea salt crystals

H O B   O R   O V E N
190°C 375°F Gas Mark 5 Roasting Oven

Peel the potatoes, cover with cold water, add the salt and bring to the boil. Cover and cook on the hob or in a preheated oven for 15-20 minutes or until tender.

Meanwhile soften the garlic in 2 table-spoons of olive oil in a pan over moderate heat for 5-8 minutes. Don't allow the garlic to change colour at all. Remove from the heat and cool slightly.

Strain the potatoes and purée through a mouli-légume or fine sieve with the garlic and oil. Add another 2 tablespoons olive oil to the garlic pan, stir in the thyme and warm gently over moderate heat to release the flavour of the herb. Stir into the puréed pota-toes, add salt and pepper to season. Spoon into a hot serving dish, cover and keep until ready to serve. Serve in spoonfuls with freshly milled pepper, some sea salt, and the remaining olive oil dribbled over the top.

RUSSIAN-STYLE POTATO AND MUSHROOM ROLL

A thick blanket of smooth potato wrapped around a savoury filling is an appealing idea capable of many variations. This is one of my favourites.

S E R V E S   4 - 6

680 g / 1½ lb floury potatoes, peeled

salt and freshly milled black pepper

55 g / 2 oz butter

2 teaspoons potato flour or 4 teaspoons of plain flour

2 egg yolks

2 teaspoons chopped fresh dill or 1 teaspoon dill seeds

browned breadcrumbs

F I L L I N G

1 shallot, peeled and chopped

1 clove garlic, peeled and finely chopped

340 g / 12 oz mushrooms, sliced

55 g / 2 oz butter

1 teaspoon potato flour or 2 teaspoons of plain flour

55 ml / 2 fl oz single or double cream

salt and freshly milled pepper

freshly grated nutmeg

O V E N
190°C 375°F Gas Mark 5 Roasting Oven

Boil the potatoes in salted water until cooked. Drain and purée through a mouli-légume on its finest setting (or a fine sieve) into a mixing bowl. Season with black pepper and mix in the butter, flour and almost all the egg yolks. Taste to check the seasoning and stir in the chopped dill or seeds. Leave to cool a little to make it easier to handle.

Meanwhile make the filling: cook the shallot and garlic with the mushrooms in the butter until softened. Blend the flour with the cream and stir into the pan. Cook, stirring all the time, until slightly thickened. Season with salt, pepper and nutmeg. Set aside to cool slightly. Dust a sheet of greaseproof paper with flour and roll out the potato on it to make an oblong about 30 × 20cm / 12 × 8in. Roughen the top surface a little with the prongs of a fork. Spread the filling over the top leaving a margin. Roll up from the narrow side, as for a Swiss roll, using the paper to help you. Unwrap enough to brush the top with the rest of the egg yolk and sprinkle with the breadcrumbs.

Slide the roll on to a buttered ovenproof dish or tray and bake in a preheated oven for 30 minutes until really hot. Cut into slices and serve.

~

HERB POLENTA

Serve polenta as an alternative to potatoes to accompany grilled and roast meat and game. In Cottage Economy, *first published in 1821, William Cobbett recommends baking polenta covered with a layer of grated cheese.*

SERVES 4

255 g / 9 oz instant polenta cornmeal
500 ml / 18 fl oz boiling water
1 large clove of garlic, peeled and crushed with a little salt
1 teaspoon chopped sage leaves
1 teaspoon chopped parsley
1-2 tablespoons olive oil
30 g / 1 oz knob of butter
Maldon salt flakes
coarsely milled black pepper

OVEN
220°C 425°F Gas Mark 7 Roasting Oven

In a mixing bowl, add the polenta in a thin stream to the boiling water, stirring all the time until smooth. Mix in the garlic, sage and parsley. Spoon the polenta into an oiled ovenproof dish. Smooth with a fork leaving a slightly rough surface, and drizzle the remaining olive oil over the top.

Bake in the preheated oven for 20 minutes. Then rub the butter over the top and bake or place under a hot grill for an extra 5 minutes, until the top is golden brown. Sprinkle the salt and pepper over the top and serve cut into wedges.

~

Spring Vegetables
baked with herb butter

*The first pickings of spring vegetables – green
pencil-slim beans, slender carrots, a
handful of tiny broad beans or mangetout
peas and thinnings of baby leeks –
are often too few to be served separately.
But baked together, with
herb butter in a paper envelope, they retain
all their sprightly flavours and
beautiful textures.*

Serves 4

450 g / 1 lb mixed spring vegetables – all slimmer
than finger width

4 bay leaves

115 g / 4 oz butter

2-3 tablespoons chopped parsley, chervil,
tarragon and chives

a squeeze of lemon juice

salt and freshly milled pepper

Oven
200°C 400°F Gas Mark 6 Roasting Oven

Prepare the vegetables by washing, peeling
and trimming as necessary. Juicy, fresh
young vegetables straight from the garden
can be cooked as they are, larger or older
specimens may need to be par-cooked by
steaming for 4-5 minutes.

Spread 4 sheets of baking parchment on a
chopping board and make a neat pile of vegetables on each. Tuck a bay leaf in each pile.
Blend the butter with the herbs and a
squeeze of lemon juice, season to taste.
Divide the butter between the vegetables
dotting it over them in small pieces. Fold the
paper to enclose the vegetables and secure it
so that the melted butter cannot escape. I
usually resort to using wooden clothes pegs
to secure the paper during the cooking.

Place the vegetable parcels on a baking
sheet and cook in the preheated oven for 10-
25 minutes depending on their nature. Carefully transfer the parcels to 4 individual hot
plates and serve straight away.

Broad Beans with pancetta

Serves 3 - 4

85 g / 3 oz pancetta, diced

2 tablespoons olive oil

3 spring onions, chopped

350-450 g/12-16 oz broad beans, shelled

2-4 tablespoons chicken stock or dry white wine

salt

a little extra olive oil

1 teaspoon summer savory or oregano, chopped

Oven
190°C 375°F Gas Mark 5 Roasting Oven

Fry the pancetta until the fat runs. Add the
onions, beans and stock. When boiling, cover
and transfer to the oven. Cook for 10-15
minutes. Add olive oil and the herbs to serve.

Right
Spring Vegetables baked with
herb butter

GLAZED JERUSALEM ARTICHOKES
WITH WALNUTS

*The slightly smoky flavour of
Jerusalem artichokes makes a good foil for
butter-tossed walnuts.*

SERVES 4

450 g / 1 lb Jerusalem artichokes
salt and freshly milled black pepper
85 g / 3 oz butter
bay leaf
55 g / 2 oz walnut halves
1 tablespoon walnut oil
a few fine shreds of lemon zest
a little finely chopped fresh parsley

OVEN
190°C 375°F Gas Mark 5 Roasting Oven

Scrub the artichokes in cold water. Cover with cold water and bring to the boil. Simmer for 4-5 minutes or just long enough to be able to peel off their skin. If time is short, peel the artichokes when raw – but, of course, you lose some of the vegetable in the peelings – and cook in boiling salted water with a splash of milk to keep them white.

Cut the artichokes into walnut-size pieces and season lightly with salt and pepper. Melt two-thirds of the butter in a casserole or ovenproof dish, add the artichokes and stir until coated with butter. Add the bay leaf, cover and bake in the preheated oven for 15 minutes or until tender.

Melt the remaining butter, and slightly brown the walnuts over moderate heat.

Remove the bay leaf and stir the walnuts into the artichokes with the walnut oil. Sprinkle the lemon zest and parsley on top and serve.

FRENCH GREEN BEANS
WITH GARDEN HERBS

To be cooked in butter rather than water,
haricots vert *need to be very young
and tender – ideally freshly-picked from
the garden.*

SERVES 4

340 g / 12 oz slim French beans
30 g / 1 oz unsalted butter
1 tablespoon mixed chopped fresh herbs –
parsley, chives and chervil or tarragon
sea salt crystals

OVEN
180°C 350°F Gas 4 Roasting Oven

Rinse the beans in cold water, drain well and trim the ends. If very slim, leave the beans whole, otherwise cut into short lengths. Melt the butter in a cast-iron skillet or frying-pan, add the beans and toss gently until coated with butter. Place buttered paper over the beans, place in a casserole dish and transfer to the oven for 10-20 minutes until tender. Remove the paper, stir in the chopped herbs and sprinkle the salt over the green beans. Serve straight away, from the cooking dish if you wish.

ASPARAGUS CRACKERS

An admirable way of making the most of a handful of freshly-cut asparagus.

S E R V E S   3 - 4

12 short stems of asparagus or asparagus tips
55 g / 2 oz unsalted butter
½ teaspoon basil or tarragon leaves, chopped
a squeeze of lemon juice
salt and freshly milled pepper
12 sheets of filo pastry, 18 × 13 cm / 7 × 5 in
24 chive stems (optional)

O V E N
200°C 400°F Gas Mark 6 Roasting Oven

If necessary, trim the stalks (reserving them for soup) from the asparagus to leave 10 cm / 4 in tips. Briefly blanch the asparagus in boiling salted water for 3-4 minutes until almost cooked. Drain and refresh in cold water, drain well on kitchen paper.

Melt the butter with the chopped basil or tarragon and the lemon juice, season to taste. Take a piece of filo pastry, brush with the herb butter and place an asparagus tip in the centre lengthways and brush with plenty of butter. Roll up the pastry like a Christmas cracker, pinching it together at each end of the asparagus, and if you wish securing it by tying with a chive stem. Place the asparagus parcels on a buttered non-stick baking sheet and brush them with any remaining butter.

Bake in the preheated oven for 8-12 minutes until the pastry is golden. Serve warm with drinks or a summer soup.

ROASTED BABY LEEKS

Derived from a dish first tasted in San Francisco, this way of cooking baby leeks reveals their true – almost asparagus-like – character.

S E R V E S   3 - 4

225-340 g / 8-12 oz baby leeks, trimmed and washed
a handful of bay leaves
55 g / 2 oz butter
coarsely crushed coriander seeds
½ teaspoon finely grated zest of lime or orange
a little lime or orange juice
salt

O V E N
200°C 400°F Gas Mark 6 Roasting Oven

Steam the baby leeks over a layer of bay leaves in a steaming basket for 5-10 minutes until tender.

Melt the butter in a cast-iron skillet or ovenproof dish large enough to hold the leeks in a single layer. When foaming, add the coriander seeds and the leeks turning them over until coated with butter. Cover with buttered paper and cook in the preheated oven for about 10 minutes or until just changing colour.

Remove from the oven, sprinkle with the grated zest and juice of the lime or orange and some salt. Serve the baby leeks either hot or warm.

ONIONS
BRAISED IN BEAUJOLAIS

Autumn crops of pickling onions coincide nicely with the season's Beaujolais, they make an excellent combination when cooked together.

SERVES 4

450 g / 1 lb small onions, pickling size

55 g / 2 oz butter

generous pinch of ground allspice

½ teaspoon potato flour

300 ml / 10 fl oz Beaujolais or other fruity red wine

2 bay leaves

a sprig of thyme

salt

a little brown sugar – depending on the wine

OVEN
180°C 350°F Gas Mark 4
Roasting or Baking Oven

Peel the onions. Melt the butter in a cast-iron casserole, add the onions and cook for 4-5 minutes, stirring from time to time, until they are just changing colour and the onions are well coated with butter. Stir in the allspice, blend the potato flour with the wine and add to the onions with the bay leaves and thyme. Season lightly with salt and bring the mixture back to the boil, stirring continuously.

Cover with a tight-fitting lid and transfer the casserole to the preheated oven. Cook for 30-40 minutes until the onions are tender but not mushy. Transfer to the hob, taste the sauce and if too sharp add a little sugar. Bubble the sauce until slightly thickened. Serve with game and roast meats.

BRAISED CELERY HEARTS

Braised celery has a most appetizing flavour, it makes a particularly good accompaniment to game dishes.

SERVES 4

4 celery hearts

salt and freshly milled pepper

30-55 g / 1-2 oz butter

OVEN
190°C 375°F Gas Mark 5 Roasting Oven

Wash and, if necessary, trim away any tired or discoloured ends of celery stalk. Plunge the hearts in boiling, salted water and cook, covered for 8-10 minutes. Drain well and reserve the cooking liquor for soups. Transfer the celery to a buttered ovenproof dish, season with pepper and dot the remaining butter on top. Cover with a tight-fitting lid or a sheet of foil secured round the edge of the dish.

Bake in the preheated oven for 20-30 minutes or until the celery is tender and the butter has browned.

Left
ONIONS BRAISED IN BEAUJOLAIS

AUBERGINES
ROASTED WITH CUMIN AND FRESH GINGER

Roasted aubergine shrinks during the cooking but the roasting intensifies the flavour wonderfully.

SERVES 6

3 large aubergines

6 tablespoons sunflower oil

2 cloves of garlic, peeled and chopped

1 teaspoon cumin seed

4 cm / 1½ in piece of fresh ginger, peeled and grated

salt

2 tablespoons lemon juice, or to taste

OVEN

180°C 350°F Gas Mark 4
Roasting or Baking Oven

Wipe the aubergines with a damp cloth, then cut them into long strips and into pieces about 2.5cm / 1in long. Heat the oil in a roasting tin and stir in the garlic and cumin seed. Cook for about 3 minutes over moderate heat then add the aubergine slices and stir until the vegetable has absorbed the oil.

Roast the aubergine in the preheated oven for about 30 minutes or until the aubergine is cooked, stirring from time to time. Five minutes before serving, stir in the ginger and add salt and lemon juice to taste.

Transfer to a hot serving dish and serve plain or with some cool yoghurt spooned on top and sprinkled with chopped coriander.

~

BRAISED LETTUCE

A Victorian recipe that works best with a Victorian variety of lettuce – the close-hearted Little Gem.

SERVES 6

3 Little Gem lettuces

85 g / 3 oz butter

2 tablespoons sherry or tarragon vinegar

OVEN

180°C 350°F Gas Mark 4 Roasting Oven

Trim the lettuce stalks, discard any limp or discoloured outer leaves and, if necessary, wash in cold water and drain well. Cut each lettuce in half lengthwise.

Melt two-thirds of the butter in a casserole dish large enough to hold the lettuces in a single layer. When the butter is foaming, add the lettuces and turn over until coated with butter. Then place them cut side down and cover with a lid or buttered paper.

Cook in the preheated oven for 10-15 minutes or until they are cooked but not mushy.

Transfer the lettuces to a hot serving dish. Add the vinegar to the dish and mix with the cooking juices. Simmer for 1 minute, add the remaining butter and as soon as it is melted pour or spoon the sauce over the lettuces and serve.

~

Right
AUBERGINES ROASTED WITH CUMIN AND FRESH GINGER

AUSTRIAN RED CABBAGE
WITH APPLE

The most delicious slow-cooked red cabbage dish I know, and one that improves with reheating.

S E R V E S   4 - 6

1 small red cabbage

30 g / 1 oz butter

1 small onion, peeled and chopped

3-4 ripe dessert apples such as Cox's Orange Pippin, cored and chopped

3 tablespoons red wine vinegar

30 g / 1 oz sugar

salt

¼ teaspoon ground allspice or ½ teaspoon caraway seeds (optional)

a little hot water

O V E N

160°C 325°F Gas Mark 3 Simmering Oven

Discard any damaged outer leaves of the cabbage. Quarter and remove the stalk, then finely shred the rest.

Melt the butter in a cast-iron casserole and stir in the onion. Cook until softened then add the cabbage, apples, vinegar, sugar and a little salt. Stir well, then add the ground all-spice or caraway seeds if desired and enough hot water to a depth of 1 cm / ½ in.

Cover with a tight-fitting lid and cook in the preheated oven for 45-60 minutes.

Serve with roast meat and game.

SAVOY CABBAGE
STUFFED WITH CHESTNUTS
AND CRANBERRIES

The French classic of chou farci, *given an autumnal stuffing to suit vegetarian guests.*

S E R V E S   3 - 4

1 medium-sized Savoy cabbage

C H E S T N U T   S T U F F I N G

450 g / 1 lb fresh chestnuts, oven-roasted or boiled and peeled

85 g / 3 oz butter

1 shallot, peeled and chopped

1 clove garlic, peeled and chopped

115 g / 4 oz cranberries

½ teaspoon finely grated zest of orange

juice of an orange, strained

½ teaspoon finely chopped fresh thyme

¼ teaspoon ground allspice

salt and freshly milled black pepper

4 tablespoons dry white wine

4 tablespoons vegetable stock or water

O V E N

180°C 350°F Gas Mark 4
Roasting or Baking Oven

Discard any damaged outer leaves from the cabbage, then cut the stalk level with the leaves and cut a cross in it. Wash the cabbage well under cold running water and place in a steamer set over simmering water. With the lid slightly open, steam the cabbage for 5-7 minutes or until a knife can be pushed easily into the centre. Lift out the cabbage and leave it to cool slightly.

To make the stuffing, chop the chestnuts finely – in a processor if you wish. Melt two-thirds of the butter in a pan and soften the shallot and garlic for 3-4 minutes, not allowing it to change colour. Stir in the cranberries and the orange zest and juice, and cook for 5 minutes. Then stir in the chestnuts, thyme, allspice and some salt and pepper and remove from the heat.

Gently fold back the cabbage leaves until you reach the yellow heart, then carefully cut away 1-2 tablespoons of the heart to enlarge the hollow. Spoon in the chestnut stuffing and fold the outer leaves back into place to enclose it. If necessary, secure the cabbage parcel with string.

Place the stuffed cabbage in a casserole, add the remaining butter, wine and stock and cover with a tight-fitting lid. Cook in the preheated oven for 30-40 minutes. Transfer the cabbage to a serving plate, remove the string and serve the cabbage cut into wedges with the cooking juices.

≈

WINTER VEGETABLE HOTPOT

A delicious and sustaining winter dish for herbivores that's been known to satisfy even ardent meat-eaters. Vary the ingredients of this vegetable hotpot according to availability and your particular preference.

SERVES 4

55 g / 2 oz butter
1-2 cloves of garlic, peeled and thinly sliced
2 onions, peeled and sliced
4 carrots, scrubbed or peeled and sliced

½ small swede, peeled and chopped
2 parsnips, peeled and sliced
2 turnips, peeled and sliced
4-5 Jerusalem artichokes, scrubbed or peeled and sliced
½ head celeriac, peeled and cut into shreds
1 leek, washed and chopped
salt and freshly milled black pepper
2 tablespoons chopped fresh herbs, especially parsley and thyme
450 g / 1 lb potatoes, peeled and thinly sliced
1 tablespoon flour

OVEN
190°C 375°F Gas Mark 5
Roasting or Baking Oven

Melt half the butter in a 2 litre / 3½ pint casserole and tilt to coat the base. Add the garlic and arrange all the vegetables except the potatoes in layers, seasoning them lightly with salt and pepper and sprinkling them with chopped herbs as you go. Arrange the sliced potatoes in overlapping circles on top. Blend the flour with 1-2 tablespoons of cold water to make a paste, then stir in a further 300 ml / 10 fl oz of cold water and pour the smooth mixture over the vegetables. Dot with the remaining butter and cover the casserole with a tight-fitting lid.

Cook in a preheated oven for 1-1½ hours or until the potatoes are cooked. Remove the lid for the last 10 minutes to brown the top layer of potatoes.

As a variation, just before serving, scatter 55-115 g / 2-4 oz diced or grated Lancashire or Wensleydale cheese over the potatoes and place under a hot grill until melted.

≈

BAKED BEETROOT
WITH TARRAGON

Baking, rather than boiling, intensifies the flavour and colour of beetroot. The vegetable has an affinity with tarragon and tastes particularly delicious served hot with tarragon and chive butter.

SERVES 4-6

900 g / 2 lb small, young beetroot – ideally straight from the garden

1 teaspoon mild salad oil

55 g / 2 oz unsalted butter

1 teaspoon chopped tarragon leaves

1 teaspoon chopped chives

sea salt crystals

OVEN

180°C 350°F Gas 4 Roasting Oven

Cut the stalks from the beetroot – if the beetroot are freshly pulled then the leaves can be cooked and served just like spinach – leaving an inch or so attached. Wash the beetroot in plenty of cold water, taking care not to break the skin, then drain well. Brush the oil over the inside of a lidded cast-iron casserole and add the beetroot in a single layer. Cover and cook in the oven for 1-2 hours depending on size, then remove from oven.

Leave uncovered for 4-5 minutes or until the beetroot are cool enough to handle. Peel the beetroot and arrange, whole or cut into quarters, in a hot serving dish. Melt the butter in a small pan, stir in the herbs, pour over the beetroot, sprinkle with salt and serve.

❧

BAKED SWEETCORN
WITH MEXICAN BUTTER

Quite the most delicious way of cooking cobs of sweetcorn – though they must be very fresh and juicy for the best results.

SERVES 4

4 young cobs or heads of sweetcorn

85 g / 3 oz slightly salted butter, softened

½-1 small clove of garlic, peeled and crushed

½-1 small red hot chilli pepper, deseeded and finely chopped

1-2 tablespoons coriander leaves, chopped

salt and freshly milled black pepper (optional)

OVEN

200°C 400°F Gas Mark 6 Roasting Oven

Strip the leaves and the silks from each cob. Place each cob on baking parchment or foil large enough to enclose it. Blend the butter with the garlic, chilli pepper and chopped coriander. The proportion of each is a matter of personal preference. Spread the seasoned butter over the sides of the corn cobs. Wrap securely in the sheets of paper or foil and place on a baking sheet.

Bake in the preheated oven for 20-30 minutes depending on size. Transfer to hot individual plates and serve as a separate course, accompanied by any remaining butter and bread to soak up the juices.

❧

Right
BAKED BEETROOT WITH TARRAGON

Roasted Sweet Peppers
with Sesame Seed Dressing

*Sweet peppers are one of the most
versatile and well-flavoured of vegetables.
They go specially well with an
oriental dressing.*

S E R V E S   4

4 large sweet peppers – choose from red, green,
orange, yellow
2-3 tablespoons light sesame oil
2-3 teaspoons red rice vinegar
2 tablespoons toasted sesame seeds

O V E N
200°C 400°F Gas Mark 6 Roasting Oven

Wash the peppers, then using a sharp cook's
knife, cut them in half and remove the stalks,
seeds and any surplus membrane. Cut them
into narrow strips, ideally with pointed ends.
Heat a large casserole dish and spread out
the peppers in a thin layer. Roast in the preheated oven for 20-30 minutes, turning the
peppers over now and again, until they are
changing colour at the edges.

Transfer the peppers to a hot serving plate.
Pour the sesame oil into the hot pan and
place over high heat. Stir in the vinegar and
allow the mixture to bubble for a minute.
Remove the pan from the heat and stir in the
sesame seeds. Immediately spoon the dressing over the peppers and serve. Accompany
with plain rice and / or grilled meat.

~

Afghanistan Okra Salad

*An Afghanistani student living in England
introduced me to this appetizing dish.*

S E R V E S   6 - 8

450 g / 1 lb okra
2 tablespoons sunflower oil
1 medium onion, peeled and finely chopped
½ teaspoon cumin seed
450 g / 1 lb tomatoes, peeled and roughly
chopped
1 teaspoon sugar
salt and freshly milled black pepper
150 ml / 5 fl oz Greek style goats' or sheeps' milk
yoghurt
2-3 tablespoons finely chopped mint
squeeze of lemon juice

O V E N
190°C 375°F Gas Mark 5 Roasting Oven

Trim the stalk end of each okra pod and
rinse them in cold water, then drain well.
Heat the oil in a large skillet and soften the
onion over moderate heat. Add the cumin,
tomatoes, sugar, salt and pepper and cook,
stirring for 5 minutes. Add the okra and
spoon the tomato sauce over them.

Cover the skillet with a sheet of foil and
cook in the preheated oven for 20-30 minutes, spooning the sauce over the okra
halfway through the cooking time.

Spoon the okra into a serving dish and if,
necessary, reduce the sauce over high heat
for a few minutes. Then spoon over the okra
and serve hot or cold, spooning the yoghurt
mixed with the mint and lemon over the top.

~

Lentil Salad with Anchovies and Black Olives

Balanced with other richly-flavoured ingredients such as anchovies and olives, the grey-green lentils of Le Puy make a fine salad, substantial enough as a main course or – served in smaller portions – as a distinctive start to a meal. Delicious all the year round.

Serves 4

225 g / 8 oz Le Puy lentils

1 bay leaf

1 clove garlic, peeled and sliced

Anchovy Dressing

2 anchovy fillets from a 70 g / 2½ oz tin of anchovy fillets

1 clove garlic, peeled

6 tablespoons olive oil

2 teaspoons sherry vinegar

½ teaspoon freshly ground coriander

freshly milled black pepper

1 teaspoon finely chopped parsley

finely grated zest of ½ lemon

salt to taste

Garnish

some red-flushed oak leaf lettuce and other russet salad leaves

the remaining anchovy fillets (see below)

100 g / 3½ oz black olives (pitted)

1 tablespoon flat-leaf parsley

Oven

140°C 275°F Gas Mark 1 Simmering Oven

Tip the lentils into a cast-iron casserole, add the bay leaf, garlic and 600 ml / 1 pint cold water and bring to the boil on the hob. Cover and cook in the preheated oven for 25-30 minutes. The lentils are cooked when they are soft but not mushy and they have absorbed almost all of the liquid.

Remove the casserole from the oven and set aside to cool slightly. Make the dressing by chopping the two anchovy fillets, place in the bowl of a processor or blender and add the garlic, olive oil, vinegar, coriander, pepper and parsley. If necessary, add salt to taste. Whizz to a smooth sauce and pour over the lentils. Stir in the lemon zest and set aside the lentils at room temperature for 2-3 hours before serving.

When ready to serve, arrange the lettuce leaves around the edge of a shallow serving dish and spoon the dressed lentils into the centre. Place the remaining anchovy fillets and the olives on top, and garnish with the parsley leaves.

CHAPTER 8

DESSERTS
AND
PUDDINGS

*It is sometimes said that England's true
genius in cooking is for the sweet
dishes that bring a meal to a close. The
delicate syllabubs and creams,
the fruit tarts and pies, the scented jellies
and sorbets, often date
from centuries ago.*

Left
CLYST WILLIAM BARTON APPLE
TART *page 144*

THE SPIRIT of many of these dishes derives from the Elizabethan kitchen when the English fondness for sweet, spiced and scented dishes flowered into the beautiful concoctions found in the manuscript recipe books of manor houses throughout the land.

A high proportion of these receipts – the older term for recipes – is still usable today. But look at the diversity of ingredients used in this domestic cooking of the past – angelica leaves and gillyflowers, rose petals and apricots, elderflower and lemon balm, all home-grown in the kitchen gardens of the cooks themselves. And we see our true culinary heritage.

While it is true that the most perfect fruit such as a white peach or a dessert fig should be picked at its peak of ripeness and eaten straight away, this is a counsel of perfection that is not always achievable. Even those of us who do, at times, produce ambrosial fruit from the garden also have to deal with the more plentiful crops of commonplace apples, pears and plums, not to speak of the reproachful baskets of their windfalls that rot quickly enough unless dealt with by cooking.

And then, of course, some fruits such as quinces and damsons, and the cooking varieties of pears, have to be subjected to heat in order to be palatable.

But the joy of cooking fruit in an oven is the intensity of flavour that develops in the absence of water, or when, instead, fruit is baked or poached with a few spoonfuls of fruit juice or butter, cream or wine. Furthermore, oven-cooked fruit is spared the turbulence of hob-boiling which can reduce acid fruit such as rhubarb and gooseberries to a formless pulp the moment you turn your back on them.

Our English climate with its damp equable weather almost requires the existence of hot, warming puddings. Baked sponge puddings turned out and served with a steaming zesty sauce, and hot fruity crumbles and pies that recapture the glorious bounty of summer harvests, are some of our finest traditional dishes. For a decade or so this kind of homely food has been under-rated, but now that the wheel of fashion has brought English country cooking back into favour, let us hope that, this time, it will be realized that these things are too good to forget.

MANGO, PEAR AND PAPAYA *EN BRIOCHE* WITH PASSION-FRUIT *SABAYON*

*I devised this pudding for a small birthday
dinner because buttery* brioches
*filled with hot fruit makes a very good
combination. A quick and easy version of this
recipe is to bake slices of* brioche *in
the oven, then arrange the fruit on top and
spoon over the sauce.*

SERVES 4

4 small Parisienne-style *brioches*

55 g / 2 oz unsalted butter

45 g / 1½ oz caster sugar

1-2 tablespoons Poire William liqueur

½ teaspoon finely grated zest of lemon or orange

1 ripe mango, peeled and diced

1 ripe dessert pear, peeled and sliced

1 papaya or pawpaw, peeled, deseeded and
diced

4 × 25 cm / 10 in squares of baking paper

4 × 20 cm / 8 in lengths of paper ribbon

PASSION-FRUIT *SABAYON*

2 ripe passion-fruit

2 tablespoons Sauternes or a sweet white wine
like Montbazillac

55 g / 2 oz caster sugar

4 egg yolks

OVEN
190°C 375°F Gas Mark 5 Roasting Oven

Cut a slice from the top of each *brioche* and
reserve as lids. Use a teaspoon to scoop out
the centre from each *brioche* leaving a wall
just over 1 cm / ½ in thick.

Melt the butter with the sugar, liqueur and
zest of lemon or orange. Add the prepared
fruit and toss gently until covered with butter.
Divide the fruit between the *brioches* and
spoon over any remaining buttery juices.
Replace the top on each *brioche* and place in
the centre of a square of baking paper. Bring
the four corners of the paper together and
secure by tying with the ribbon. Place the
four paper-wrapped *brioches* on one large or
four small *gratin* dishes and bake in the preheated oven for 15-20 minutes until the
brioches and fruit are piping hot.

Meanwhile make the *sabayon*. Cut the passion-fruit in half and scoop the flesh and
seeds into a bowl placed over simmering
water. Add the wine, sugar and egg yolks
and whisk for 5-10 minutes with a hand-held
electric whisk until the mixture is light and
frothy. Remove from the heat and spoon into
a warmed jug.

Serve the *brioches* still in their paper
wrappings. Untie the ribbon and spoon the
passion-fruit *sabayon* into each *brioche*.

~

LITTLE ORANGE FLOWER CUSTARDS

I find just a small serving of a nicely-judged pudding helps to induce that marvellous feeling of well-being experienced at the end of a good meal.

SERVES 4-6

30 g / 1 oz caster sugar

150 ml / 5 fl oz freshly squeezed orange juice

2 eggs

2 egg yolks

2 teaspoons orange flower water

150 ml / 5 fl oz *crème fraîche*

½ teaspoon finely shredded orange zest

OVEN

180°C 350°F Gas Mark 4
Roasting or Baking Oven

Stir the caster sugar into the orange juice until dissolved. Beat the eggs and egg yolks with the orange flower water and whisk in the orange juice. Strain the mixture into 4-6 small ovenproof dishes and place in a bain-marie or a roasting tin of warm water.

Cover the dishes with a sheet of cooking foil and bake in the preheated oven for 20-30 minutes or until the custards are set. Remove from the oven and when cool transfer to a cold place until ready to serve. Just before serving spoon a little *crème fraîche* on top of each custard and sprinkle with shreds of orange zest.

∽

BAKED AMARETTI-FILLED NECTARINES

Smooth-skinned nectarines are usually juicier and more flavourful than peaches, moreover they do not need to be peeled for this lovely Italian-inspired dish. A perfect summer dessert.

SERVES 8

8 ripe nectarines

100 g / 3½ oz day-old sponge cake

8 Amaretti biscuits

2-3 tablespoons orange or almond liqueur like Cointreau or Amaretto

4 tablespoons Italian vermouth or a sweet white wine

1 tablespoon caster sugar

OVEN

180°C 350°F Gas 4 Roasting Oven

Wash the nectarines in cold water and dry on a cloth. Starting at the stalk end cut each nectarine in half and gently remove the stones. In the food processor reduce the cake and Amaretti biscuits to fine crumbs, add the liqueur and whizz until the mixture binds together. Divide into 8 portions and sandwich each nectarine with the mixture, gently squeezing the two halves together so that a band of filling is showing. Place in an ovenproof dish and add the wine. Sprinkle the caster sugar over the fruit.

Bake for 20-30 minutes until the fruit is *just* cooked. Cool slightly and serve warm or chilled with pouring cream if you wish.

∽

SOUFFLE OMELETTE WITH SUMMER FRUIT

My preference is for fresh morello cherries but raspberries, strawberries or blackcurrants, or a mixture of them all works equally well.

SERVES 4

340-450g/12oz-1lb ripe soft fruit, ready to cook
100g/3½oz caster sugar or according to taste
2 tablespoons sweet white wine or water
1 teaspoon potato flour
4 large (size 2) eggs, separated
30g/1oz vanilla sugar
1 teaspoon plain white flour
1 teaspoon icing sugar

OVEN
200°C 400°F Gas Mark 6 Roasting Oven

For soft fruit, simply toss with the sugar and divide between 4 small buttered *gratin* dishes. Firm fruit such as cherries (remove the stones first) and gooseberries need to be cooked with the sugar and half the wine or water until soft. To thicken the mixture, blend the potato flour with the remaining wine or water and stir into the hot fruit for 1 minute. Then divide between the buttered *gratin* dishes.

Whisk the egg whites until stiff then fold in the vanilla sugar. Cream the egg yolks with the flour and fold into the egg whites. Spoon the soufflé mixture over the fruit.

Bake in the preheated oven for 8-12 minutes or until the soufflé has risen and is golden brown. Dust the tops of the dishes with sifted icing sugar and serve straight away.

RASPBERRY SOURED CREAM SOUFFLE

Quick and easy to make, this kind of low-altitude soufflé never fails. The raspberries cook to a fragrant sauce under the fluffy soufflé.

SERVES 4

small knob of butter
225g/8oz raspberries
1 tablespoon Grand Marnier or Cointreau
85g/3oz caster sugar
1 tablespoon cornflour
3 large (size 2) eggs, separated
150ml/5fl oz soured cream
1 teaspoon finely grated zest of orange
1 teaspoon icing sugar

OVEN
190°C 375°F Gas Mark 5 Roasting Oven

Butter the sides of a 20cm/8in diameter fluted flan dish. Arrange the raspberries evenly over the base and spoon over the liqueur. Mix two-thirds of the sugar with the cornflour and stir into the fruit.

Whisk the egg whites until stiff and stir in 1 teaspoon caster sugar. Beat the egg yolks with the rest of the sugar, the soured cream and the zest of orange until pale. Fold in the egg whites and spoon over the fruit.

Bake in a preheated oven for 15-20 minutes until set and the top is golden brown. Remove from the oven and dust the top with the icing sugar shaken from a fine sieve. Serve straight away.

SAN FRANCISCO COCONUT CREAM

This is my version of a delightful pudding that I first tasted in San Francisco.

S E R V E S 6

400 g / 14 oz tin of coconut milk

pinch of ground cinnamon

45 g / 1½ oz vanilla-flavoured caster sugar

2 eggs

2 egg yolks

3 ripe passion-fruit or 2-3 tablespoons demerara sugar

O V E N

190°C 375°F Gas Mark 5 Roasting Oven

Shake the tin of coconut milk well so that the cream mixes with the milk. Open the tin and pour the milk into a pan, stir in the cinnamon and sugar over moderate heat. Gently whisk the eggs with the egg yolks in a bowl. Stir in the coconut milk and strain the mixture into six 85 ml / 3 fl oz cocotte dishes.

Place the dishes in a roasting pan of warm water and bake in the preheated oven for 20-30 minutes until just set in the centre. Remove from the oven and set aside to cool. Chill and just before serving spoon the seeds and flesh of half a passion-fruit on top of each coconut cream. Alternatively, sprinkle the demerara sugar on top of each chilled cream and place under a very hot grill until the sugar has melted. Set aside until cool then serve plain or with with small crisp almond biscuits.

ROASTED FRESH FIGS WITH HONEY AND WINE

An ambrosial way of preparing fresh figs.

S E R V E S 4

12 ripe figs

knob of butter

2 tablespoons clear lavender honey or 30 g / 1 oz caster sugar

2-4 tablespoons sweet Muscat wine such as Rivesaltes or Beaumes de Venise

O V E N

200°C 400°F Gas Mark 6 Roasting Oven

Wash and dry the figs – I find this is wise even if freshly picked since insects love ripe figs. Rub the butter over the inside of a shallow ovenproof dish. Halve the figs and arrange in the dish in a single layer, cut side up. Drizzle the honey (or sprinkle the sugar) and wine over the fruit.

Bake in the preheated oven for 15-20 minutes until the figs are cooked and the juices are a bubbling syrup. Serve straight away with *crème fraîche*.

Right
ROASTED FRESH FIGS WITH HONEY AND WINE

RUM AND PECAN PIE

If you prefer, this tart can be made with walnuts instead of the more subtly-flavoured pecan nuts. Walnuts, however, are more characteristic of the cooking of the West Country where you can find ancient gnarled walnut trees still flourishing in old cottage gardens in sheltered coastal regions.

SERVES 6-8

PASTRY

170 g / 6 oz plain white flour

30 g / 1 oz caster sugar

85 g / 3 oz unsalted butter

1 egg yolk

finely grated zest and juice of ½ orange

FILLING

170 g / 6 oz shelled pecan nut halves

3 tablespoons dark Jamaican rum

85 g / 3 oz butter

85 g / 3 oz dark muscovado sugar

1 large egg

2 generous pinches of ground allspice or ground cinnamon

OVEN

200°C 400°F Gas Mark 6 Roasting Oven

180°C 350°F Gas Mark 4
Roasting or Baking Oven

Sift the flour and sugar into a bowl, rub in the butter until the mixture resembles bread-crumbs. Mix to a dough with the egg yolk blended with the orange zest and juice. Roll into a ball, wrap in a plastic bag and chill for 15-30 minutes. Then roll out the dough and line a buttered 23 cm / 9 in flan tin (loose bottomed), using a fork to prick the pastry base all over. Bake in the preheated oven – at the higher temperature – for 10-15 minutes until lightly coloured.

Meanwhile make the filling. Chop half the pecan nuts fairly finely and mix with the rum. Cream the butter with the sugar until light and fluffy, beat in the egg and ground allspice or cinnamon. Fold in the chopped pecans and rum, and spoon the mixture into the tart case. Spinkle the remaining pecan nuts on top. Bake the tart in the preheated oven – at the lower temperature – for 20-25 minutes. Transfer to a plate and serve warm or cold with *crème fraîche* or thick sweetened cream flavoured with Jamaican rum.

CLYST WILLIAM BARTON APPLE TART

This is the most recent variation of an apple tart that I often bake here, using our own apples. Adding cream and eggs to an apple, or codling, tart appears in seventeenth century English cooking, and is still common practice in the country cooking of France.

SERVES 6

PASTRY

150 g / 5 oz flour

30 g / 1 oz vanilla-flavoured caster sugar

pinch of salt

85 g / 3 oz butter

1 egg yolk

FILLING

18 Amaretti biscuits, crushed into crumbs

450-680 g / 1-1½ lb ripe eating apples, peeled and sliced

55-85 g / 2-3 oz sugar, depending on the sweetness of the fruit

150 ml / 5 fl oz double or clotted cream

2 tablespoons Muscat or elderflower wine

2 eggs, beaten

½ teaspoon vanilla essence or orange flower water

OVEN

200°C 400°F Gas Mark 6 Roasting Oven

180°C 350°F Gas Mark 4
Baking or Roasting Oven

Sift the flour, sugar and salt into a bowl, and rub in the butter. Mix to a dough with the egg yolk and 2-3 tablespoons ice-cold water. If the pastry is still very cold, roll out to line a 23 cm / 9 in pie dish about 5 cm / 2 in deep. Otherwise chill the pastry first.

Spread three-quarters of the biscuit crumbs over the pastry base and cover with the sliced apples, sprinkling them with sugar as you go. Use a balloon whisk to mix the cream with the wine, eggs and vanilla essence and pour over the apples. Sprinkle the remaining biscuit crumbs on top.

Bake in the preheated oven, at the higher temperature, for 20 minutes. Then bake for a further 10-15 minutes, (ideally) at the lower temperature, until the pastry is golden and the custard has set. Cool slightly and serve warm or cold.

BUTTERED PEARS

A lovely dish, made in a trice, that produces its own caramelized sauce. Ripe, well-flavoured dessert apples can be prepared in the same way though they may take a little longer to cook.

SERVES 4

4 large, ripe, firm dessert pears

55 g / 2 oz unsalted butter

30 g / 1 oz caster sugar

1-2 tablespoons of Poire William, rum or Madeira

OVEN

200°C 400°F Gas Mark 6 Roasting Oven

Peel, core and quarter the pears. Cut into thick slices. Melt the butter in a large cast-iron skillet or frying-pan, and when it is foaming add the pears. Turn the slices over in the butter and sprinkle in the sugar. Cook over high heat for 2 minutes then transfer to a casserole dish in the preheated oven for 6-8 minutes. The pears are ready when just changing colour and the caramel sauce is thick and syrupy.

Transfer the pears to one large or 4 small warm plates. Add the liqueur to the pan, boil up and then spoon over the pears. Serve straight away with pouring cream.

Devon Pear Dumplings
with Pineau de Charentes

The poet Samuel Coleridge – who lived in nearby Ottery St Mary – is claimed to have said that 'a man cannot have a pure mind who refuses apple-dumplings'. I feel much the same about this pear version.

Serves 4

4 ripe dessert pears

2 tablespoons dry white wine or the juice of ½ lemon

55 g / 2 oz white marzipan

3 teaspoons red Pineau de Charentes

225 g / 8 oz all-butter puff pastry

1 egg yolk or milk, to seal and glaze

16 cloves

1-2 tablespoons caster sugar

a small piece of lemon zest (optional)

½ teaspoon arrowroot

Oven

200°C 400°F Gas Mark 6 Roasting Oven

Wash and dry the pears. Thin-skinned pears such as Red Williams can be left unpeeled, otherwise peel thinly reserving the peelings and leaving the stalk intact. Use a vegetable knife to carefully remove the core from each pear from the base, still keeping the pear whole. If peeled, brush the pears with wine or lemon juice to prevent discolouring. Blend the marzipan with 1 teaspoon of the Pineau de Charentes and spoon this into the core cavity of each pear.

Roll out the pastry to make 4 squares each large enough to enclose a pear. Brush the pastry edges with egg yolk or milk and draw up the corners to meet at the stalk. Secure each corner with a clove and press the edges firmly together. Brush the pastry with egg yolk and place on a baking sheet covered with non-stick baking paper. Bake in a pre-heated oven for 25-30 minutes, until the pastry is puffed up and golden and the pears are cooked throughout.

Meanwhile make a sauce by placing the pear cores and any reserved peelings in a pan with the remaining dry white wine or lemon juice. Add the sugar, lemon zest and 150 ml / 5 fl oz water. Simmer gently for 5 minutes. Discard the pear peelings and lemon zest. Add the arrowroot blended with the remaining Pineau de Charentes and cook, stirring for 1-2 minutes, until thickened. Serve the sauce while still warm, with the pear dumplings and, if desired, accompany with Devonshire clotted cream.

Right

DEVON PEAR DUMPLINGS WITH PINEAU DE CHARENTES

Fluffy Wholemeal Pancakes
with cherries

*This is a supper-in-the-kitchen
pudding, best suited to small numbers and
served straight from the pan.*

Serves 4

225 g / 8 oz sweet cherries (stoned), raspberries
or strawberries

sugar to taste

½ teaspoon arrowroot or potato flour (optional)

2 large (size 2) eggs, separated

115 ml / 4 fl oz milk

55 g / 2 oz wholemeal flour

good pinch of ground allspice

30 g / 1 oz dark muscovado sugar

small knob of butter for the pan

150 ml / 5 fl oz *crème fraîche* or soured cream

Hob or Oven
190°C 375°F Gas Mark 5 Roasting Oven

Prepare the cherries, or other fruit, by lightly
cooking in the oven or on the hob with
sugar to taste. If the mixture is too liquid,
thicken it by blending the potato flour with a
tablespoon of water or wine, mix into the
fruit and cook, stirring until thickened. Keep
the fruit warm.

Mix the egg yolks with the milk and gradually beat in the flour, ground allspice and
sugar. Whisk the egg whites until stiff and
fold into the batter mixture. Heat a 15-
18 cm / 6-7 in cast-iron omelette pan, add a little butter and tilt the pan to run it over the
base. Spoon in a quarter of the batter and
spread across the pan evenly. Cook on the
hob or in the oven until the top of pancake

is set, turn over the pancake and cook in the
same way until golden brown. Repeat for
other pancakes.

Transfer to a hot plate, spoon over some
of the warm cherries and top with a spoonful
of *crème fraîche*.

Light wholemeal pancakes also go well
with BUTTERED PEARS (page 145) or with
fruits preserved in alcohol such as mandarin
oranges or spiced peaches.

Galette des Rois

*Traditionally baked for Twelfth Night, this
pastry should contain a bean which entitles
the finder to be 'king for the night' and
have his every command obeyed. During the
rest of the year, when the tart is
cooked without the bean, it is known as
Gâteau Pithiviers.*

Serves 6-8

400 g / 14 oz prepared-weight puff pastry

55 g / 2 oz butter, softened

85 g / 3 oz caster sugar

85 g / 3 oz ground almonds

1 egg yolk

2 tablespoons dark Jamaican rum

1 dried bean (optional)

a little beaten egg

1 tablespoon icing sugar

Oven
220°C 425°F Gas Mark 7 Roasting Oven
200°C 400°F Gas Mark 6
Roasting or Baking Oven

Divide the pastry in half and roll each piece into a circle 20 cm / 8 in across. Place one pastry circle on a slightly dampened non-stick baking sheet.

Blend the butter with the caster sugar, ground almonds, egg yolk and rum. Spread over the pastry base, leaving a generous margin to brush with beaten egg. If using the bean drop it on to the filling. Place the other circle of pastry on top, pressing the edges together, and brush with beaten egg. Leave the *galette* for 5 minutes then using the point of a knife mark a diamond trellis pattern on it, and cut a small steam vent in the centre.

Bake in a preheated oven for 10 minutes then lower the temperature and bake for a further 30 minutes, when the pastry should be risen and golden. Dust the icing sugar through a sieve over the *galette* then place under a very hot grill until the sugar has caramelized and is golden and glistening. For the best flavour, serve the *galette* warm.

❧

PLUM AND ALMOND RATAFIA CRUMBLE

Baked in an old-fashioned enamel pie dish, this is a pudding that tempts even the most dedicated dieter.

SERVES 6

570 g / 1¼ lb ripe plums
115-170 g / 4-6 oz caster sugar – depending on the sweetness of the fruit
2 teaspoons cornflour

100 g / 3½ oz small almond ratafia biscuits
225 g / 8 oz plain white flour
115 g / 4 oz demerara sugar
150 g / 5 oz butter
good pinch of ground cinnamon

OVEN
180°C 350°F Gas Mark 4
Roasting or Simmering Oven

Halve the plums and discard the stones. Measure the caster sugar and cornflour into a plastic bag and shake carefully until mixed. Add the plum halves and shake gently until the fruit is coated with sugar. Turn the contents of the bag into a deep enamel or ceramic pie dish that holds 2 litres / 3½ pints. Cover the fruit with buttered paper and bake in the preheated oven for 10-15 minutes or until the fruit is half-cooked then discard the buttered paper.

Meanwhile tip the almond ratafia biscuits into the plastic bag and crush lightly with a rolling pin until reduced to coarse crumbs. Measure the flour and demerara sugar into a mixing bowl and rub in the butter. Stir in the ground cinnamon and all but 2 tablespoons of the ratafia crumbs. Spoon the mixture over the fruit in an even layer and sprinkle the reserved ratafia crumbs on top. Bake for 25-30 minutes or until the crumble is cooked and the top is golden brown. Serve hot or warm with cream.

For variation, in place of plums, use 450 g / 1 lb chopped pink rhubarb mixed with 225 g / 8 oz fresh or frozen raspberries.

❧

Fresh Lime Tart

*Fresh limes give this fruit curd tart a subtle
tangy flavour.*

SERVES 6

PASTRY

150 g / 5 oz plain flour

70 g / 2½ oz caster sugar

85 g / 3 oz unsalted butter, softened

2 egg yolks

1 drop of vanilla essence

LIME CURD FILLING

3 limes

100 g / 3½ oz caster sugar

3 eggs

55 g / 2 oz unsalted butter, melted

OVEN

200°C 400°F Gas Mark 6 Roasting Oven

180°C 350°F Gas Mark 4
Roasting or Baking Oven

To make the pastry, sift the flour and sugar on to a cold work-surface or into a chilled wide bowl. Make a well in the centre and add the butter and egg yolks mixed with the vanilla essence. Use the fingertips to gradually blend all the ingredients together. When the mixture starts to resemble breadcrumbs, press it together to form a ball of dough. If you have time, rest the pastry in a cold place, wrapped in plastic or under the upturned bowl, for 30 minutes. Then roll out to line a buttered 23 cm / 9 in fluted tart tin (with a loose bottom). Prick the pastry base all over and place on a hot baking sheet in the preheated oven for 8-10 minutes until the pastry is set and starting to change colour.

Remove the pastry case from the oven and cool slightly. Meanwhile wash and dry the limes. Cut a thin strip of peel from 1 lime and cut into long narrow shreds. Place in a pan and cover with cold water. Bring to the boil and simmer for 5-7 minutes until tender. Drain well, toss in a little caster sugar and set aside on kitchen paper in a warm place.

Grate the remaining zest from the limes and mix with the strained juice of the fruit. Beat in the eggs, the remaining sugar and the melted butter. Pour the filling into the slightly cooled pastry case and replace in the oven preheated to the lower temperature for 20-25 minutes until set. Cool the tart for 5 minutes then carefully transfer to a flat serving plate, decorate with the sugared zest of lime and serve while still warm or when cold.

Hot Chocolate Sauce

*The favourite sauce of chocolate fanciers, for
spooning over vanilla ice cream and cream-
filled profiteroles or meringues.*

MAKES 500 ML / 18 FL OZ

200 g / 7 oz best-quality plain chocolate

3 tablespoons strong black coffee

1-2 tablespoons dark rum or brandy (optional)

300 ml / 10 fl oz double cream
a pinch of ground cinnamon

OVEN

120°C 250°F Gas Mark ½ Simmering Oven

Break the chocolate into pieces and place in the top half of a double boiler or in an ovenproof bowl standing in hot water. Add the remaining ingredients, cover with a lid of a plate and place in the preheated oven for 20-30 minutes or until the chocolate has melted. Stir until smooth and serve hot.

~

MARMALADE PUDDING
WITH ORANGE CARDAMOM SAUCE

A timeless baked sponge pudding with a zesty buttery sauce.

SERVES 4

knob of butter

225 g / 8 oz well-flavoured coarse-cut orange marmalade

115 g / 4 oz unsalted butter, softened

55 g / 2 oz caster sugar

2 eggs

150 g / 5 oz self-raising white flour

¼ teaspoon ground coriander (optional)

generous pinch of ground mace or nutmeg

¼ teaspoon finely grated zest of orange or lemon

SAUCE

the juice of 3 large sweet oranges, strained

2 teaspoons potato flour or cornflour

3 green cardamom pods, bruised

½ teaspoon long shreds of orange zest

sugar to taste

2 tablespoons orange liqueur or Cointreau

45 g / 1½ oz unsalted butter

OVEN

180°C 350°F Gas Mark 4
Roasting or Baking Oven

Use the knob of butter to grease the inside of a 0.75 litre / 1¼ pint enamel or ceramic pie dish. Spread half of the marmalade over the base. Spoon the remaining marmalade into the bowl of a food processor and add the butter, sugar, eggs, flour and spices. Mix until fairly smooth, stir in the orange zest and spoon into the prepared pie dish. Smooth level and bake in the preheated oven for 30 minutes or until cooked in the centre with a golden brown crust.

Meanwhile make the sauce. In a small pan, blend a little of the strained orange juice with the potato flour, then add the remaining juice, the cardamom pods and orange zest. Cook together over moderate heat, stirring all the time until the sauce has thickened. Remove from the heat, taste and if necessary add sugar to taste. Cover the sauce and keep warm. Just before serving extract and discard the cardamom pods, add the liqueur and stir in the butter until melted.

Run the blade of a knife around the edge of the pudding to free it and turn out on to a serving plate. Spoon the sauce over the top and serve.

~

JOHN FARLEY'S RICH RICE PUDDING

Rice pudding was once a delectable treat, as illustrated by this exotically-flavoured version adapted from John Farley's The London Art of Cookery *first published in 1783.*

SERVES 4

450 ml / 15 fl oz full cream milk

55 g / 2 oz pudding rice

short stick of cinnamon

2 tablespoons of double cream

55 g / 2 oz caster sugar

approximately ¼ small nutmeg, freshly grated

3 teaspoons rosewater

1 whole egg

2 egg yolks

OVEN

160°C 325°F Gas Mark 3 Simmering Oven

190°C 375°F Gas Mark 5
Baking or Roasting Oven

Bring the milk almost to the boil. Pour on to the rice and the cinnamon stick in a 900 ml / 1½ pint ovenproof dish. Cover with foil and cook in a low or Simmering Oven for 45-60 minutes until the rice is tender and the mixture is thick.

Remove the cinnamon stick and stir in the cream, sugar, nutmeg and rosewater and allow to cool slightly. Beat the egg with the egg yolks and stir into the rice. Place in a

Left

JOHN FARLEY'S RICH RICE PUDDING

bain-marie or a roasting tin filled with warm water. Leave uncovered if you like a skin on rice pudding otherwise replace the foil.

Bake in the preheated oven – at the higher temperature – for 30 minutes or until just set. Serve hot, warm or chilled.

VANILLA TRIFLE CUSTARD

Genuine vanilla-scented egg custard – use in trifles or as a sauce for hot fruit dishes.

MAKES 450 ML / 15 FL OZ

150 ml / 5 fl oz single cream

300 ml / 10 fl oz whole milk

8 egg yolks

55 g / 2 oz caster sugar

vanilla essence

Heat the cream with the milk in a heavy-based saucepan or a double-boiler until almost boiling. Whisk the egg yolks with the sugar in a bowl. Pour the liquid on to the mixture, whisking all the time. Return the custard to the pan and cook stirring, taking care that the mixture does not boil or curdle, until the custard thickens. I find mixing fast with a balloon whisk also helps to ensure that the custard remains velvety smooth.

Remove from the heat and immediately plunge the base of the pan into a bowl of very cold water to stop the custard from cooking further. Stir occasionally while it cools, and flavour with drops of vanilla essence.

SCOTCH WHISKY, GINGER AND ALMOND TRIFLE

*I devised this for some Scottish friends
who visited us bearing gifts of
their local brew. The alliance of Scotch
whisky and thick Devon cream
works especially well, and makes a good
pudding for a party.*

S E R V E S 8

85 g / 3 oz sponge cake, preferably home-made

55 g / 2 oz preserved ginger, thinly sliced

30 g / 1 oz blanched almonds, flaked or cut in
slivers and toasted

6 tablespoons of whisky – Macallan works well

4 tablespoons ginger syrup (from the preserved
ginger jar)

500 ml / generous ¾ pint vanilla-flavoured trifle
custard (see recipe on previous page)

1 teaspoon orange flower water

2 rounded tablespoons bitter orange marmalade

W H I S K Y   S Y L L A B U B

100 ml / 3½ fl oz Muscat wine

3 tablespoons whisky

juice of ½ sweet orange

55 g / 2 oz caster sugar

300 ml / 10 fl oz double cream

Break the sponge cake into pieces and arrange in a 1.4 litre / 2½ pint glass dish. Reserve some ginger and almonds for decorating the trifle later and sprinkle the rest over the sponge cake. Mix 4 tablespoons of the whisky with the ginger syrup and drizzle over the sponge cake. Prepare the custard and stir in the orange flower water. Pour over the sponge cake and set aside in a cold place for 4-6 hours.

Warm the marmalade with the remaining 2 tablespoons of whisky and press through a sieve. Pour over the custard in an even layer.

To make the whisky syllabub, measure the wine, whisky and orange juice into a bowl and stir in the sugar until dissolved. Add the cream, whisking all the time, until thick enough to hold its shape. Spoon into mounds on top of the marmalade layer. Decorate with the reserved sliced ginger and almonds and leave in a cold place for up to 4 hours before serving.

CREME CARAMEL

*This irresistible yet inexpensive classic
displays the virtues of French
country cooking – moderation and
judgement.*

S E R V E S   4 - 6

100 g / 3½ oz granulated white sugar

600 ml / 1 pint whole milk

30 g / 1 oz vanilla sugar

½ vanilla pod-split lengthways

2 eggs

2 egg yolks

O V E N

180°C 350°F Gas Mark 4
Roasting or Baking Oven

Dissolve the sugar in 85 ml / 3 fl oz water in a small heavy-based pan over low heat. Raise the heat and boil the syrup until it turns golden brown – do not let it darken or the caramel will be bitter. Remove from the heat, cool slightly then pour into a warm ¾ litre / 1¼ pint straight sided ovenproof dish. Tilt the dish to coat the base and sides and stand it in a bain-marie or roasting tin half-full of warm water.

Heat the milk with the vanilla sugar and the vanilla pod, stirring to dissolve the sugar and distribute some of the vanilla seeds, until lukewarm. Whisk the eggs and egg yolks lightly together in a bowl. Remove the vanilla pod from the milk and pour on to the eggs, whisking lightly all the time. Strain the mixture into the caramelled dish.

Bake, covered with a sheet of foil, in the preheated oven for about 45 minutes. The custard is cooked when just wobbly but not liquid in the centre. Cool in the bain-marie then chill until ready to serve.

Just before serving run the blade of a knife around the rim of the custard to free it from the dish then carefully unmould it on to a flat plate deep enough to contain the syrup.

To make individual puddings, coat the insides of six small cocotte dishes with the hot caramel, and add an extra egg white to the custard to set it more firmly. Bake for 25 minutes or until set.

∿

ICED MOCHA SOUFFLE

This ice cream has a lovely flavour and can be served straight from the freezer.

S E R V E S   6 - 8

4 tablespoons ground filter coffee, preferably Kenyan
150 ml / 5 fl oz full cream milk
115 g / 4 oz best quality plain dessert chocolate
2 egg whites
115 g / 4 oz caster sugar
150 ml / 5 fl oz double cream

H O B   O R   O V E N
140°C 275°F Gas Mark 1 Simmering Oven

Measure the coffee and milk into a small pan and heat slowly until very hot. Cover and leave to infuse in a preheated oven for 10 minutes. Then strain the coffee milk into a heatproof bowl. Add the chocolate, broken in pieces, cover and replace in the oven for 5-10 minutes or until melted. Remove from the oven, stir until combined and set aside to cool slightly.

Meanwhile whisk the egg whites with the sugar in a mixing bowl set over simmering water for about 5 minutes or until the meringue holds its shape. Remove from the heat and continue to whisk for 3 minutes.

Whisk the cream until stiff and glossy, then carefully stir in the coffee / chocolate mixture. Fold into the meringue and spoon into a lidded plastic container. Freeze for 4-6 hours until firm.

∿

Chocolate *Marquise* with *Creme Anglaise*

This requires the best chocolate you can find. I sometimes make only the dark chocolate and serve it with the vanilla cream.

Serves 8

DARK CHOCOLATE *MARQUISE*

200g/7oz bitter-sweet dessert chocolate

100g/3½oz unsalted butter, softened and cut into pieces

3 eggs, size 3, separated

½ teaspoon ground coffee

1 tablespoon dark rum or brandy

WHITE CHOCOLATE *MARQUISE*

150g/5oz good-quality white chocolate

30g/1oz unsalted butter, softened in pieces

1-2 tablespoons white rum or kirsch

1 egg white

CRÈME ANGLAISE

2 large egg yolks

15g/½oz caster sugar

300ml/10fl oz full cream milk

½ vanilla pod, split open

DECORATION (OPTIONAL)

shaved chocolate curls

Oven (OPTIONAL)

160°C 325°F Gas Mark 3 Simmering Oven

Lightly butter a 700ml/1¼ pint non-stick loaf tin and line with baking parchment. To make the dark chocolate *marquise*, melt the chocolate in a bowl, in the oven or over hot water. Remove the bowl from the heat and add the butter. When melted stir in the beaten egg yolks and coffee mixed with the rum. Whisk the egg whites until stiff and fold into the chocolate mixture. Spoon one third of the mixture into the cake tin, smooth level and chill until almost set.

Meanwhile melt the white chocolate in a bowl, in the oven or over hot water. Remove from the heat and stir in the butter until melted then add the white rum. Whisk the egg white until stiff and fold gently into the chocolate mixture. Spoon half the mixture over the layer of dark chocolate and chill until firm. Continue to make contrasting layers of chocolate, ending with dark chocolate. Chill until firm.

To make the *crème anglaise*, beat the egg yolks with the sugar. In a double boiler or a heavy-based pan, heat the milk with the vanilla pod, stirring. Bring almost to the boil, remove the vanilla and pour on to the egg and sugar mixture. Return the sauce to the pan and cook gently for 4-5 minutes, stirring all the time, until slightly thickened. The sauce will spoil if boiled. Remove from the heat and pour into a small mixing bowl. Cover with a saucer to prevent a skin forming and set aside to cool.

To serve, wrap the tin in a hot damp cloth. Slip a knife blade between the parchment and the tin to loosen the *marquise*, then turn it out on to a flat surface. Peel off the parchment, then use a long-bladed knife dipped in hot water to cut the *marquise* into slices. Serve each slice on an individual plate with *crème anglaise* spooned around it and decorate, if wished, with shaved chocolate curls.

∾

Right
CHOCOLATE *MARQUISE* WITH
CRÈME ANGLAISE

INDEX